Streets
of the
Near West Side

(Second Edition)

By

William S. Bike

Edited by Cindy Richards

1stBooks - rev. 01/04/02

Lori L. Grove contributed to the Maxwell Street chapter. Anne M. Nordhaus-Bike contributed to the Racine Street chapter. Cover photo courtesy of the Italian American Collection, Special Collections, University Library, University of Illinois at Chicago.

iii

CONTENTS

Dedicated to the memory of

Don C. Piemonte
1960-1996

who represented everything that is good
about the Near West Side of Chicago.

Introduction

Great cities are created in two ways—physically, through the architecture their builders choose, and emotionally, through the memories and aspirations of the both the residents and the city leaders.

The streets of the Near West Side have been the thoroughfares down which a great deal of Chicago's history has traveled. The port of entry for many of Chicago's immigrant populations since the 1850s, the Near West Side traditionally has been an important gateway to America itself for 150 years.

The area includes Maxwell Street, until recently the immigrants' "Street of Dreams," on which an investment in a pushcart and good sales patter could lead a new arrival on the path to becoming a millionaire. The Near West Side also saw the beginning of the Great Chicago Fire in 1871, was the home base of organized crime in Chicago in the early part of the century, and originated the science of social work through the activism of Jane Addams and Hull House. It has always been the place where the city invented itself, tore itself down, and rebuilt itself again.

Street names reflect both the memories and the aspirations of the city's residents and builders. Thoroughfares are named for those of the past whom people warmly remember (several streets in the area were named for 19th century presidents of the United States, well-respected and beloved individuals whose achievements were still fresh in Chicagoans' minds), and also for aspirations for a better future (Reuben Street was changed to Ashland, for example, when residents hoped to evolve from "rubes" to landed gentry).

As it was from its inception and is today, in 1983 the Near West Side was one of the hottest areas in the city for news. Home to the Illinois Medical Center and its several hospitals, UIC, Little Italy/Taylor Street, controversial land acquisitions, and some of the most corrupt politics in the city, the Near West Side was a community in which a journalist couldn't walk down the street without stumbling over a potential front-page story. Yet curiously the area had been without a newspaper since the *Near West Side Gazette* folded in 1971. Not only were there no publishing chains operating a newspaper in the area, but no independents seemed willing to take a gamble there, either.

That changed when Mark J. Valentino, a lifelong resident of the 1500 block of Polk Street and son of a *Chicago Tribune* truck driver, decided to invest his small savings into an effort to revive the old independent. A 1980 graduate of DePaul University who had served as editor of its student newspaper *The DePaulia,* Valentino, at age 26, started up a new newspaper and appointed himself editor and publisher. He shortened the old name to *Near West Gazette,* and invited Dismas Fernandez, one of the editors of the previous *Gazette,* and William S. Bike, another former *DePaulia* editor, to be his associate editors.

The *Near West Gazette* first was published on May 5, 1983. The Near West Side has never been the same, as the *Gazette* has become the most important vehicle that brings the diverse neighborhoods it covers together, filling a void that existed despite the communities' close proximity. After years of scoops, public service, and journalism and community activism awards, the newspaper, now called the *Near West/South Gazette* to reflect its expansion to Chicago's South Loop area, still is owned and operated by Valentino and still is going strong.

Between Dec. 15, 1983, and June 3, 1993, Bike wrote a column for the *Gazette* entitled "Streets of the Near West Side," revealing the generally unknown origins of the names of the streets with which Near West Siders otherwise are so familiar. Most of the histories in this book came from those columns, and from new material added for both the 1996 and 2001 editions.

Streets' 1996 edition proved extremely popular, garnering nationwide print acclaim and local broadcast publicity. Chicago Alderman Burton Natarus introduced a resolution honoring Bike for writing *Streets of the Near West Side,* which was passed by the Chicago City Council at its June 1997 meeting. The book was named "UIC Today Online Book of the Week" for two weeks running in June and July that year. And in 1998, Bike's publicity efforts for the book received a Grand Award from Communications Concepts, a journalism and public relations think-tank based outside Washington, DC.

"The 1996 press run of *Streets* sold out pretty quickly," Bike notes. "That's what's most meaningful to me. Official honors are appreciated, but the vote of confidence of the readers, many of whom have contacted me to tell me how much they have enjoyed the book, has been the greatest reward of all."

As the Near West Side continues to reinvent itself, we hope you will use and enjoy the second edition of *Streets of the Near West Side* as your guidebook for years to come.

1st Books
October 2001

Aberdeen Street

(1100 west)

Aberdeen Street takes its moniker from the chief seaport and largest city in northeastern Scotland. It is the capital of the county of Aberdeenshire.

Famous now for its haddock and cod fishing industries, Aberdeen historically was one of the seats of revolutionary movements attempting to achieve independence for Scotland from England. Because of this, King Edward III of England burned the city in 1336. The parts of the city that survived the inferno are called Old Aberdeen; New Aberdeen comprises the rest.

The city is situated on a strip of land about 1.5 miles wide between the Don and Dee Rivers, two waterways that allow easy access into the scenic Scottish Highlands.

Known as the "Granite City" because almost all of its buildings are made of pale granite dug from nearby quarries, the city contains many churches dating from the 14th century. Points of interest include the "Auld Brig o' Balgownie," a bridge built in the early 1300s across the Don River, and the University of Aberdeen.

Ada Street

(1326 west)

Ada Street is named for a woman who was so astute at managing her money that, at her death in 1938, she left a total of $2,250,000 depression-era dollars. She bequeathed the money to various deserving non-profit organizations in the Chicago area, as well as to some of her relatives.

Mrs. Ada Sawyer Garrett was the granddaughter of Justin Butterfield, an attorney who once defeated Abraham Lincoln for the post of land commissioner of Illinois. In 1834, Butterfield bought 80 acres of land around and including the area now known as Logan Square, located on the Northwest Side of Chicago.

Butterfield had three daughters, known in 19th century Chicago high society as "the beautiful Butterfield girls." Daughter Elizabeth married Dr. Sidney Sawyer, and the couple had their own daughter, Ada. Ada grew up to be a popular society debutante, and she married T. Mauro Garrett, a railroad official.

It was Mrs. Sawyer and Mrs. Garrett who were instrumental in subdividing the land Butterfield had purchased in the Logan Square area, creating what was then a genteel neighborhood of mansions, as well as adding to the family's fortune.

When her husband died in 1900, Mrs. Garrett went into seclusion, devoting her time to managing her estate. Finances occupied her time for the next 27 years, until she succumbed to illness.

She lived another 11 years, dying in 1938 at the age of 82. She left money to the Chicago Historical Society, the Art Institute, the University of Chicago, a number of hospitals, and several homes for the poor, for the disabled, and for orphans.

Adams Street

(200 south)

He liked to swim in the Potomac River in the nude. He became president of the United States in 1825 despite having come in second in the election. Scrupulously moral and honest, he was accused of being a pimp and a corrupt politician. Adams Street, located at 200 south and stretching from the South Loop west across the entire city, is named for him: John Quincy Adams, the sixth president of the United States.

Adams was the son of the second president, the revolutionary hero John Adams, and so a life in government service was just a continuation of the family business for him. He served superbly in a wide variety of diplomatic posts, and as President James Monroe's Secretary of State formulated the Monroe Doctrine, which ordered European powers to stay out of the affairs of the Western Hemisphere and was the cornerstone of American foreign policy.

Adams ran for president in 1824. This was the first presidential contest in which none of the heroes of the American Revolution was a candidate, so several individuals were vying for election. General Andrew Jackson got the most electoral votes, but not a majority. Adams came in second.

According to the U.S. Constitution, if no candidate receives a majority, the House of Representatives chooses a president. When it met to do so early in 1825, one key New York Congressman, Stephen Van Rensselaer, just did not know what to do. So he closed his eyes, bowed his head in prayer, and asked for Divine guidance. When he opened his eyes, he saw a scrap of paper on the floor with Adams' name on it. Figuring a vote for Adams was therefore God's will, Van Rensselaer cast his ballot accordingly. This swung the New York delegation, and the election, to Adams.

Some votes from Congressman Henry Clay's friends also were vital in electing Adams, and when Adams made Clay secretary of state, charges of a "corrupt bargain" rang from sea to shining sea.

The Adams presidency, because of its manner of inception, faced much public hostility and therefore achieved little. The next election was the first negative presidential campaign in U.S. history. Jackson forces accused Adams of everything from the "corrupt bargain" to having

3

procured the sexual services of a woman for the Czar of Russia during one of Adams' diplomatic missions there. Adams' forces, not to be outdone, accused Jackson of everything from being a descendant of slaves to having an illegal marriage. Adams lost.

As president, the normally stuffy Adams did engage in one surprising extravagance. He would get up at four a.m. to swim in the nude in the Potomac River. Once, an enterprising female reporter who had been rebuffed in several attempts to get an interview with the president sat on his clothes on the river bank and refused to give them up until he agreed to talk to her.

Adams' post-presidential career, like Jimmy Carter's, is proof that an unpopular presidency does not preclude a successful life. In 1830, some of Adams' neighbors asked him to run for Congress. He did, and served there for 17 years. The old patriot strongly defended the right of petition and opposed slavery and became one of Congress' most important and beloved members. His congressional speeches earned him the nickname "Old Man Eloquent."

Adams collapsed and died in the House of Representatives in 1847, prompting a colleague to comment, "Where could death have found him but at the post of duty?"

Until George W. Bush, John Quincy Adams had been the only son of a former president to become president himself. The elder George Bush in 2001 gave his presidential son the nickname "Quincy."

Ashland Avenue

(1600 west)

The naming of Ashland Avenue represents one of the more unusual stories in choosing a street's designation. For Ashland Avenue is not named for a person or a town; it is named for a house.

The house, located not in Chicago but in Kentucky, belonged to a man who ran for president three times and lost each time. The street was named for the house because of an insult.

Ashland had originally been named Reuben Street after a prominent real estate investor named Reuben Tayler. Since Chicago already had a similarly named thoroughfare with a slightly different spelling, the Taylor Street that had already been named for President Zachary Taylor, the Chicago City Council used Reuben Tayler's first name to honor him.

In the latter half of the 19th century, the street that is now Ashland was the main thoroughfare of what was then the equivalent of Chicago's "Gold Coast." The boulevard was lined with stately mansions, opulent churches, and parks. One had to be quite rich to live on Reuben Street.

Close to Reuben Street were the slums of the Near West Side. Poor people used to come over to Reuben Street to gape at and to insult the rich people living there. The insult heard most often was, "Hey, Rube!"

Being called a rube was quite offensive to people of that era, so the wealthy residents of Reuben Street petitioned the City Council to change the street's name.

Many of the well-to-do living on the street had come from Kentucky to Chicago to make their fortunes. They were admirers of Henry Clay, who was one of the most influential politicians of the first half of the 19th century and a native of Kentucky. Clay's Kentucky home and estate were called Ashland.

To the street's residents, the name Ashland represented the qualities they admired in their neighborhood: stateliness, charm, and sociability. So, this high-sounding name was given to what now is a very ordinary street.

Clay unsuccessfully ran for the presidency in 1824, 1832, and 1844. He coined the phrase, "I'd rather be right than president." His opponents felt that he was incapable of being either; his supporters believed that his

5

leadership helped hold the Union together through some of the country's most severe crises before the Civil War.

Not only was Ashland a street of stately mansions in the 19th century; it also was a street of beautiful churches, several of which remain.

At Polk Street, Ashland Avenue is home to St. Basil's Greek Orthodox Church, which was slated for demolition in the days of Near West Side urban renewal mania. Mayor Harold Washington's Department of Housing put an end to that plan and saved the church in 1985.

At 1124 S. Ashland, one finds First Immanuel Lutheran Church, built in 1888 to serve the area's huge population of German Lutherans. They moved away in the early 1900s and the area became predominantly Catholic, but through reaching out to public housing residents and college students living in the area, and by actively seeking parishioners from outside the area, including former neighborhood residents, the church continues operating.

In 1885, the Episcopal Church of the Epiphany was constructed at 201 south. Episcopal canon law allows a church building to be consecrated only after all debt is retired, so the structure was consecrated ten years later, and celebrated its centennial by launching a three-year restoration drive in 1995.

Not so fortunate was Mary Thompson Hospital at 140 north. Opened in 1865, the hospital was forced to shut down in 1988, an early casualty of America's latter 20th century health care crisis.

On a late September day that same year, a gunman named Clem Henderson rampaged up Ashland killing four people, including a female police officer, before another cop gunned Henderson down. A *Gazette* photographer was on the scene, and captured the heart-rending aftermath on film.

Bell Street

(2234 west)

In performing historical research, one finds that conflicting information shrouds relatively modern times as well as antiquity.

Although Bell received its name only about a century ago, city records conflict as to why.

The street may be named in honor of a soldier of the Civil War, George Bell (*not* to be confused with the former Chicago White Sox and Chicago Cubs outfielder). Soldier George Bell was a member of Company G of the 37th Illinois infantry, the "Fremont Rifle Regiment."

Organized by a member of the Chicago Board of Trade in the summer of 1861, the regiment trained on the city's North Side before being mustered into the army in September of that year.

During training, the regiment was given a fine silk banner by the Board of Trade. The standard featured a portrait of General John Fremont, a hero of the Mexican War, and was the reason the 37th was nicknamed for Fremont. Bell himself at the same time was presented with a sash and sword by members of the Chicago Bar Association, so he may have been an attorney.

Other sources claim that the street was named for Alexander Graham Bell, inventor of the telephone.

Bell was born in Scotland in 1847, and began his working life assisting his grandfather and father in teaching the deaf to speak. After moving to the United States in 1871, the continued to work with the deaf. One of his pupils was Mabel Hubbard, with whom he fell in love and married.

The knowledge of the principles of sound Bell gained through his work with the deaf inspired him to tinker with communications-related inventions.

In 1874 he invented a telegraph that could send two messages at once. But a year later, Bell came up with his greatest invention: the telephone.

A late entry in the Centennial Exposition (world's fair) of 1876, the telephone won the gold medal for new inventions and gained worldwide publicity. The resulting sales of the new invention made Bell financially independent for life.

Bell spent the rest of his days inventing, and he eventually worked on the phonograph, an early x-ray machine, air conditioning, and a crude helicopter, among other projects. He became a United States citizen in 1882, and died in 1922.

Bishop Street

(1438 west)

One of Chicago's leading citizens in the late 19th century, Henry W. Bishop was the first president of the Union Club of Chicago, a private association organized by 60 of the city's leading gentlemen in 1878. Bishop held the group's presidency through 1883. A judicial official, he also served as a master in chancery.

In his will, Bishop left $2.5 million to form the John Crerar Library of engineering, medical, and science texts, located at 5730 S. Ellis on the University of Chicago campus.

The 900 block of south Bishop Street has the honor of having led off the comeback of the Near West Side in the early 1970s. A block known for its chicken-wire fences, it was the first to be beautified by the city with a landscaped cul-de-sac in the middle. Neighbors tore down their chicken-wire fences, rehabbed their homes, and the rehabbing of the Near West Side was underway.

That same block also was the site of a major neighborhood controversy in late 1998 and early 1999. A neighborhood group circulated a petition to get new sewers and water lines for the street, which everyone wanted, but it contained an obscure proviso that the end of the block where the street met Taylor Street would become a plaza with a statue of baseball player Joe DiMaggio as its centerpiece.

Although everybody liked Joltin' Joe, nobody particularly wanted him blocking their street. Despite neighbors' opposition to the plaza, they couldn't fight City Hall and their street was blocked off. That made it necessary to remove the cul-de-sac in the middle of the block, and the symbolic point of origin to Near West Side rejuvenation was lost forever.

Blue Island

(diagonal)

Blue Island is a street named for an optical illusion.

During the 19th century, a ridge running south from 87th Street near Western Avenue on foggy days reminded some people of a blue-colored island appearing among the mists. The ridge, created by a glacier, is nearly 100 feet higher than Lake Michigan. It runs past the city limits at 119th St., so the founders of the suburb that begins there, Blue Island, decided to take the town's name from this ghostly topographic feature. Being an industrial bastion (Chicago's gunpowder mills moved there late in the 19th century), Blue Island's air for most of the 20th century appeared smoky and foggy no matter what the weather conditions. The Chicago street was named for the town to the south.

Built in 1854 as a plank road to connect south Western Ave. to downtown, the street became world famous during the labor struggles of the late 19th century, as workers and police frequently clashed there outside the McCormick Reaper Works. It also was an important route for farmers taking their cattle to the stockyards. Blue Island's nickname was "Black Road" after it later was paved with ebony-colored cinders.

In the 1890s, the stretch of Blue Island from 18th to 22nd St. was one of the area's busiest shopping districts—the Woodfield Mall of its day. The street also housed the city's garment trade, and a number of saloons that was unusually high even for the high-imbibing 19th century.

Blue Island no longer leads to downtown, as its northern terminus now is at the St. Ignatius College Prep campus at Roosevelt Road. Two of the three Chicago Housing Authority ABLA highrises that stood there on the south of Roosevelt in recent decades have been razed for duplexes and rowhouses for current ABLA residents and other low-income families.

Bowler Street

(630 south)

Many Near West Side area streets are named for political figures, but Bowler Street is named for a West Side political figure whose impact on the area still is apparent 35 years after his death.

James Bernard Bowler spent most of his political life in the City Council. Sworn into that body in 1906, he left finally in 1953, with hiatuses from 1923 to 1927 when he served as the city's commissioner of compensation, and in 1934 when he worked as commissioner of vehicle licenses. He was president pro tem of the council for eight years, and his 42 years in that body made him the longest-serving alderman ever.

Chicagoans having to suffer aldermen moaning about "unfair" redistricting in the early 1990s harkened back to Bowler's era as a more genteel time. Bowler was the chairperson of the council's remapping committee in 1923 when it became apparent that the fairest map would redistrict him out of his own 19th Ward. With no hesitation, he proceeded to remap himself out of the council. Four years later, he ran in the new ward in which he found himself residing, the 25th, and won.

In 1953, he became congressman for the Seventh District. Bowler is considered to have been one of the five individuals most responsible for pushing through the Congress (now Eisenhower) Expressway project. "No one man can take credit, but I'm proud to say my name belongs right up there with the others," Bowler said.

He also was instrumental in bringing to the area another important development that is vital today: the Illinois Medical Center, an area and government bureau devoted to promoting health care provision and research on the Near West Side. Bowler "was a main cog in the development of the West Side Medical Center," said the late Chicago Mayor Richard J. Daley.

Born and reared in the area, Bowler worked throughout his career to return the Near West Side/West Side to its pre-20th century glory. He died on July 18, 1957, at the age of 82 in his home at 1311 S. California Ave.

Lest one think that Bowler was a typical boring politician, he had the distinction of having been a professional bicycle racer as a young man. In his later years, he gained the nickname "The Silver Fox," and was described in his obituary in the *Chicago's American* newspaper as "one of the most colorful political figures in Chicago and Illinois for the past half century."

Cabrini Street

(820 south)

Cabrini Street is the only street on the Near West Side named for a saint.

St. Frances Xavier Cabrini was born in the town of Sant'Angelo in Lombardy, Italy, on July 15, 1850. The youngest of 13 children, she had always dreamed of becoming a nun and of doing missionary work in China.

At 13, she was sent to Arluno to study under the Daughters of the Sacred Heart, and at 18 she was certified as a teacher. Four years later she contracted smallpox, and because of this, she was refused admission into that order and into the Canossians as well. It was not until five years later, when she was teaching at an orphanage in Codogno, that she was allowed to take her vows and become a nun.

Three years after that, the local bishop closed the orphanage because it allegedly had been mismanaged. Sister Frances and seven of the orphan girls who wished to become nuns then founded the Missionary Sisters of the Sacred Heart on November 14, 1880. Mother Cabrini, as she came to be called, composed the rules and constitution of the order, and she continued as its superior-general until her death.

The order established seven homes and a free school and nursery in its first five years. Its good works brought Mother Cabrini to the attention of Bishop Giovanni Scalabrini of Piacenza and of Pope Leo XIII. They urged her to go to America to help the growing population of Italian immigrants there. She gave up her dream of working in China, and she and six other sisters came to New York in 1889.

Mother Cabrini became a United States citizen ten years later. She founded many convents, schools, orphanages, and hospitals in the United States, South America, and Europe. She and her Missionary Sisters provided health care in Chicago for a century, and the saint herself helped lay the bricks when Columbus Extension Hospital, later called St. Frances Xavier Cabrini Hospital and then Saint Cabrini Hospital, was built at 811 S. Lytle in 1911.

The story of that hospital's closing constituted the top investigative reporting effort ever undertaken by the *Near West/South Gazette.*

In 1995, Columbus-Cabrini Health System, the management of the hospital, decided to close Saint Cabrini Hospital and move its operations to St. Anthony's Hospital, another facility the system operated at 2875 W. 19th Street.

Despite Saint Cabrini Hospital's importance in Chicago history, major media in Chicago barely reported on the fight over its closure, and if they covered it at all, they played the story as the inevitable result of small hospitals being squeezed out by larger competitors.

The *Near West/South Gazette,* however, performed a public service in informing the public about the real story that the other media missed: that the hospital was not being closed through inevitability, but through a management plan that may have stretched back a year to when Columbus-Cabrini Health System acquired St. Anthony's.

Columbus-Cabrini Health System in mid-1995 endeavored to close the hospital despite a plea from doctors on staff to be allowed six months to raise the patient census, which they were confident they could do, and despite the fact that the hospital had rebounded from more dire economic straits in the past—having many of the same medical personnel, with their proven track records, on staff.

Marketing and maintenance at Saint Cabrini had been sporadic and limited since 1994, when Columbus-Cabrini Health System acquired St. Anthony's, causing speculation that the closing had been planned since then, even though Columbus-Cabrini Health System was using 1995 cuts in Medicare and Medicaid as its main public rationale for the closing.

The *Gazette* obtained closed-meeting testimony given at a confab of Columbus-Cabrini Health System managers that called into question Columbus-Cabrini Health System officials' motives. For example, while Columbus-Cabrini Health System officials publicly were saying that the cost of improvements needed for the physical plant of Cabrini was part of the reason for closing it in favor of St. Anthony's, privately they discussed at the meeting that Cabrini needed only $6 million in improvements, compared to $9 million required for St. Anthony's.

Also, the *Gazette* reported, at the meeting one of the managers said that there was a 75 percent overlap between the service areas of the two hospitals and admitted that they "did not know this" when they acquired St. Anthony's, thereby bringing two Columbus-Cabrini Health System hospitals into competition with each other for the same patients.

And, although Columbus-Cabrini Health System officials were publicly talking about the need for downsizing and consolidating as reasons for closing Saint Cabrini, the *Gazette* found out that privately one official was actually talking about building a new hospital elsewhere in the city.

In editorials, the *Gazette* performed a public service by comparing Columbus-Cabrini Health System officials' public and private statements, and by calling on Columbus-Cabrini Health System to fire the two top officials who held the greatest amount of responsibility in the decision to close Saint Cabrini.

The *Gazette* was the only news outlet to tell the public that it had a right to request a public hearing by the Illinois Health Facilities Planning Board and thereby keep the hospital open longer. Had no one requested such a hearing, the hospital could have been closed sooner. As a direct result of the *Gazette's* coverage, Chicago Alderman Burton Natarus requested a public hearing. The time it took to set it up, to hold the meeting, and for the Illinois Department of Public Health to make a ruling based on it, kept the hospital open through Jan. 19, 1996, even though management had originally wanted to stop admitting patients on Nov. 13, 1995—ironically, St. Frances Cabrini's feast day—and shut down the hospital four days later.

During the battle, *Near West/South Gazette* editor Mark Valentino became somewhat of a public figure, being perceived as the leader of the effort to keep the hospital open. *Crain's Chicago Business* considered him as such in a front page article in January, 1996.

While working in Chicago during World War I, Mother Cabrini was stricken with malaria. She died at Columbus Hospital on Dec. 22, 1917. Her body is preserved in the chapel of Mother Cabrini High School in New York City.

In 1928, a movement toward her canonization as a saint began when Cardinal George Mundelein ordered a hearing on the merits of her cause. Canonization finally occurred on July 7, 1946, and Mother Cabrini became the first U.S. citizen to be declared a saint.

Pope Pius XII said, "Although her constitution was very frail, her spirit was endowed with such singular strength that, knowing the will of God in her regard, she permitted nothing to impede her from accomplishing what seemed beyond the strength of a woman." Her feast day is Nov. 13.

Carpenter Street

(1032 west)

Carpenter Street is named for Philo Carpenter, who was Chicago's first pharmacist.

Born in Massachusetts, Carpenter came to Chicago in 1832 and opened the settlement's first drug store in a log cabin on what is now Lake Street. He made enough money in two years to afford to return to the East and marry his fiancee.

Philo and Ann Carpenter's arrival in Chicago was a small turning point in the area's history, because they came into town in a fancy carriage. This was the first pleasure vehicle to arrive in Chicago, and the Carpenters' trip in such a carriage proved that the area was safe from Indian attacks.

Carpenter invested heavily in real estate in the areas surrounding what are now LaSalle Street and Wacker Drive. But the depression of 1837 wiped him out, and his creditors took all of the land he had purchased. The area would be worth well over $100 million today.

The resilient Carpenter retained his pharmaceutical business and soon was financially solvent again. A religious man, he organized the Home Sunday School of the First Presbyterian Church. He was an elder in this church until the Civil War, when members of the congregation split over whether to support the North or the South.

He then organized a new church, the First Congregational, and became deacon. Carpenter also was a member of the Chicago Theological Seminary, and was managing director of the Chicago Bible Society.

The aftermath of the fire of 1871 saw Carpenter in another leadership role as he organized the Relief and Aid Society. He also was a member of the school board and of the board of health, and was a crusader for temperance reform. He died in 1886.

Social activist Carpenter would be pleased that on the thoroughfare named for him, at Polk Street, stands Agape House, a warming shelter for the homeless. And as a proponent of education, he also would be pleased that the street is home to the Galileo Scholastic Academy of Math and Science, whose students achieve test scores notable enough to receive national recognition.

Clinton Street

(540 west)

"I've got a mule
And her name is Sal
Fifteen miles
On the Erie Canal."

—Verse from a popular ballad, circa 1820

At the beginning of the 19th century in the United States, there were no superhighways nor railroad conglomerates. The only ways to get from the East Coast to the Midwest were by dirt road or by waterway.

Water travel was the cheapest and easiest mode of transportation in the infant nation, and if lakes and rivers didn't lead to where Americans wanted to go, then they simply dug their own rivers in the form of canals.

The granddaddy of all of America's early 19th-century canals, the one that allowed people for the first time to travel without incredible hardship to what would become Chicago, was the Erie.

And there would have been no Erie Canal without DeWitt Clinton, after whom Clinton Street is named.

Born in 1769, Clinton was a New York lawyer and political leader who, between 1789 and 1815, served in the New York State Legislature, the U.S. Senate, and as mayor of New York City.

Since the 1770s, political leaders had proposed plans for linking Lake Erie at Buffalo, N.Y., to the Atlantic Ocean via canal across New York State. Clinton took up the cause in 1810 as mayor of New York City and attempted for six years, without success, to obtain Federal funds for that project.

Supporters then advocated that the State of New York alone finance the canal, and that proposal became the one issue of the 1817 New York governor's race. Clinton ran for governor as the pro-canal candidate, and his victory brought the start of canal work that very year.

The canal was completed in 1825, and for years afterward it served as the main traffic artery between the East Coast and the Great Lakes. Without the Erie Canal, it is doubtful that the Great Lakes cities of Detroit, Milwaukee, and Chicago would have developed as they did.

17

Workers with nothing but hand tools, horses, and mules (as mentioned in the ballad) dug a canal 363 miles long, 40 feet wide at the surface, and 28 feet wide at the bottom, four feet deep and with a total of 84 locks.

The proliferation first of railroads and then highways greatly reduced the importance of the Erie and of other canals, but for a time they had been indispensable to the development of the United States.

Clinton died in 1828, living long enough to see his dream canal thrive.

Congress Parkway

(500 south)

Congress Parkway is, not surprisingly, named for the United States Congress in Washington, D.C. However, Congress Parkway, like many of the streets of the Near West Side, used to be named for a president of the United States.

Until 1872, Congress Parkway was known as Tyler Street after John Tyler, the 10th president.

Tyler's father had been Thomas Jefferson's college roommate, so the Virginian grew up with a taste of politics. Elected vice president in 1840 (the latter half of the "Tippecanoe and Tyler too" team), he was playing marbles with some of his children (he would father 16) in April, 1841, when he was informed that President William Henry Harrison had died.

No one knew what to do; no president had died in office before. It was Tyler who decided that he was now president, and it has been Tyler's precedent that has been followed ever since when a president has died or resigned.

Tyler served as president until 1845. A Southerner, Tyler supported the Confederate States in the Civil War against the United States, despite having been president of the U.S. Tyler even was elected to the Confederate House of Representatives in 1861.

His siding with the South made the City Council decide to change the name of his street, as even seven years after the war feelings were still bitter against Confederate sympathizers.

When Chicago's east-west expressway was built at 500 south in the late 1950s, it was called the Congress Expressway after the street it was displacing. In 1964, the City Council decided to name its expressways after people (surprisingly, few cities do this, preferring to use the interstate route numbers), and rechristened the Congress Expressway the Dwight D. Eisenhower Expressway.

Eisenhower, the 34th president of the United States, came up with the idea of the American interstate highway system. So, more than 90 years after one president's name was taken off of the roadway, the thoroughfare again was named for an American chief executive, and Congress Parkway is just a minor auxiliary to it.

The Chicago Cubs' "friendly confines" at one time were located on Congress Street at Throop. Then known as the White Stockings, the team played its home games there from 1885 to 1892.

The first game, played on June 6, 1885, saw the Chicago National Leaguers beat St. Louis 9-2. A total of 10,237 attended the game, with another 2,000 watching from Near West Side windows and roofs.

The St. Louis manager protested the first home-run hit there by a Chicagoan, as he claimed that the right field fence was not far enough away from home plate. The umpire tape-measured the foul line at a mere 216 feet, but that distance, according to 1885 rules, was long enough. Chicago won the pennant that year, and repeated in 1886.

One of sport's first superstars, Chicago first baseman Cap Anson, had some of his best years at the Congress Street grounds. However, Anson bears some responsibility for the segregation of major league baseball until 1947.

Two Black players, Moses "Fleetwood" Walker and Welday Walker had performed in the major leagues in 1884. However, opposition led by Anson, one of the game's most important players, helped make team owners decide to forego the controversy that surrounded fielding Black players. About 75 Blacks played for minor league teams through 1899, but eventually minor league owners also succumbed to pressure and banned Blacks.

Not to be denied a place on the diamond, Blacks formed their own teams and played each other. The clubs operated independently, but that changed when one man decided to organize them, and concurrently make Chicago the capital of Black baseball.

Andrew "Rube" Foster, who in his career pitched for as well as managed and owned the Chicago American Giants Black baseball club, convinced owners of seven other teams to join with him in forming the first Black major league in 1920. Various Black major leagues would operate until the last folded in 1960.

What really made Chicago the capital of Negro League baseball was its All-Star Games of the 1930s and 1940s. Of 19 Negro League All-Star Games played, 18 were at Comiskey Park, owned by the heirs of Near West Sider Charles Comiskey. These contests often outdrew the White major leagues' All-Star Games. That popularity is often credited for influencing major league owners to start signing Black players.

Rush-Presbyterian-St. Luke's Medical Center, one of Chicagoland's largest and most influential health care providers, is located on Congress Street. Rush is among Chicagoland's top 25 employers.

On Dec. 27, 1968, it became one of the first American institutions to perform a heart transplant, only a year after the pioneering effort in that field was performed by Dr. Christiaan Barnard in Johannesburg, South Africa. Rush celebrated its 150th anniversary in 1987.

Damen Avenue

(2000 west)

Sunday, Aug. 26, 1860, the feast of the Immaculate Heart of Mary, was a landmark day in Chicago history. On that day, the church building of Holy Family parish, the biggest structure ever built in Chicago up to that time, which for years would house the biggest Roman Catholic congregation in Chicago, was dedicated. The parish was started by the Rev. Arnold Damen, S.J., a Jesuit priest and the man for whom Damen Avenue is named.

Born in Etten-Leur, Holland, in 1815, Damen left his homeland at the age of 22 to study for the Catholic priesthood at the Jesuit novitiate in Florissant, Mo. He learned to speak English there, and was ordained a priest in 1844.

Based in St. Louis by 1856, Damen was renowned across the United States for his oratorical ability. In that year, Chicago's bishop, Irishman Anthony O'Regan, thought it would be prudent to increase non-Irish Catholics' respect for him, so he invited the famed orator to Chicago to speak on the subject. It worked, and so O'Regan offered the pastorate of a new parish to Damen. The Dutch priest himself chose the 12th Street (now Roosevelt Road) site in 1857, although the bishop preferred the much busier intersection of Madison Street and Ogden Avenue.

People thought that the parish's chances of succeeding on 12th Street were grim at best. Other than a Lutheran church and a few houses, there was not much other than prairie grass for miles around Damen's site. The parish's jurisdiction was to encompass an area of 50 square miles, only one of which contained any practicing Catholics. There was no guarantee that these Catholics would come to Damen's church. And, 1857 marked the year of the worst depression America had ever experienced up to that time, so there would be little money with which to work.

But Damen not only had formal oratorical ability; he also had the "gift of gab," as the Irish like to say, and he knew he could convince people to donate money and come to the church. When a wooden temporary church was opened on July 12, 1857, it was filled to capacity as practicing, lapsed, and former Catholics came to practice their faith. The building almost immediately had to be expanded.

So Damen knew he'd have the people to fill the permanent structure which, when opened, would be the third largest church building in America.

But before work began on the permanent church, two wings were added to the temporary church to be used as a Catholic primary school. Although the idea of a Catholic school affiliated with a Catholic church seems natural today, in 1857 it was a radical idea that had seldom before been attempted. Holy Family was the first Catholic parish in Chicago to do it, and made it work, blazing the trail for the city's present-day Catholic school system, as well as for similar systems around the country.

Damen had to scramble for money during the church's building phase, but somehow the payments always were met. The pastor had an uncanny ability to find the best workers for the cheapest price. The woodcarver who created the beautiful high altar of the church, for example, Damen chanced upon while the man loaded cigar store wooden Indians onto a wagon. Damen inquired as to the identity of the carver, the teamster replied that it was he, and Damen had his artisan.

Damen's superiors often asked him to cut back on the art and decorations for the building to save money, but Damen held a tough line. He knew that if the building were a showplace, it would anchor Catholicism in Chicago. When money really got tight, Damen would auction off his horse and buggy, knowing that eventually someone would donate another buggy and another horse to the church.

By 1858, the church structure loomed big enough on the prairie that it could be seen for miles. Visitors inquired about it as they would about the Sears Tower in a latter day. The church proved to be a magnet for Catholics from all over the area, who began to build their homes around it. Holy Family, therefore, is not only important because it provided a stable anchor for the area's Catholics, but because it opened up the commercial and residential development of the whole Near West and South sides of Chicago.

Dedication day in 1860 was considered so important that 13 bishops and archbishops from all over the country attended it. Such a gathering would be impressive even today; in 1860, it was unprecedented.

By January, 1865, Damen had overseen the completion of a new school building, making the Holy Family School the first complete Catholic school in Chicago, the equal of any public school then in existence.

Holy Family achieved another first by introducing the system to Chicago of nuns teaching school children. This is another idea that seems natural now, but at the time had been tried in America only in one other place, Dubuque, Iowa. The experiment proved to be a success, and nuns teaching children became the norm.

Damen's parish also was the spawning ground for the first successful Catholic college in the Chicagoland area. The original Catholic college in the region was the University of St. Mary of the Lake, which had gone bankrupt. St. Ignatius College, which became Loyola University, opened at Holy Family in 1870, with Damen as its first president. Today, Loyola serves over 16,000 students.

The Holy Family complex narrowly avoided destruction in the Great Fire of 1871. Damen, visiting a church in Brooklyn, N.Y., and having been informed about the fire by telegraph, prayed that the wind would shift to spare his buildings from the flames that were headed right for them. That is exactly what happened, and the structures escaped unscathed.

Damen watched the city grow up around the parish. Robey Street was renamed Damen Avenue to honor this early Chicago visionary.

Although by the 1980s the church had fallen on hard times and even closed for a while, a successful preservation and restoration effort has seen the parish become a viable hub of Catholicism once again. Damen would no doubt be pleased, as he would be to know that not only does Chicago have a street named for him, but so does Etten-Leur with its "Pater Arnold Damenstraat."

On Damen between Polk and Taylor is the Westside VA Medical Center. The federal government tried to close the facility in 1996 and 1997, which would have meant veterans would have had to obtain healthcare at the smaller and harder-to-reach Lakeside VA facility. The community and elected officials fought the plan and, despite some cutbacks and administrative changes, were able to thwart the feds and save the facility.

DeKoven Street

(1100 south)

DeKoven Street gains its fame not from the individual for whom it is named, but because it was the originating site of the most famous event in Chicago's history. For it was at 558 DeKoven Street on the Near West Side that the Great Chicago Fire of 1871 began.

Rainfall in Chicago's summer and early fall that year had been virtually non-existent. The primarily wooden buildings of Chicago had been baked dry. The poor Irish of the DeKoven Street area lived in miserable wooden shanties built as close together as possible.

During the evening of Oct. 8, a fire broke out in the barn of Mr. and Mrs. Patrick O'Leary. Although legend has it that the O'Learys' cow kicking over a lantern started the fire, it is now believed that story was created as cover for a workman or drifter whose careless use of a lantern or tobacco actually initiated the blaze. The man likely would have been lynched had the truth become known.

The fire started moving north and west, but the western wing of the flames died out as the wind shifted. Thus, although the fire originated on the Near West Side, the neighborhood was spared its destructive force.

Speeding north, the fire crossed the Chicago River on four wooden bridges spanning it. When the inferno finally was extinguished two days later, it had destroyed almost every structure in the area from Harrison Street on the south to Fullerton Avenue on the north, and from the lake on the east to the north branch of the Chicago River on the west.

Some 17,000 buildings had been consumed by the fire. In addition, 250 people had died, and another 100,000, almost a third of the city's population, were left homeless.

Some Americans reflected that because Chicago had been such a raucous city, with a wide-open reputation for gambling, drinking, and other pleasures, the fire had been a punishment from Heaven, and that like the ancient cities of Sodom and Gomorrah, Chicago would never rise again.

They were wrong. Chicagoans almost immediately began reconstructing their city, creating a safer one than before with non-combustible building materials. The rebuilding attracted laborers and architects from all over the world, and many of them decided to stay permanently, increasing the city's population substantially. With the opportunity to experiment, they created the world's first skyscrapers a few years later.

By 1875, almost no evidence of the tragedy remained. Today, the only pre-fire building left in the burned district is of course the Water Tower, located at Michigan and Chicago.

The site of the O'Leary property now is home to the Chicago Fire Department training academy.

The street actually is named for banker John DeKoven (1833-1898). DeKoven came to Chicago from Connecticut in 1854 and eventually founded the Northern Trust Co. and another bank that became part of Continental Illinois National Bank and Trust Co. He also was a director of railroad companies.

Desplaines Street

(630 west)

Marketing professionals have for several years used the term "heartland" for the area most people call the Midwest. Geographers employ yet another term for the area composed of Illinois, Indiana, Iowa, Michigan, Minnesota, Missouri, Wisconsin, and parts of Kansas, Nebraska, North Dakota, Ohio, and South Dakota. This term, the "North Central Plains," inspired the name of Desplaines Street.

"Des plaines" is French for "the plains," and the term was used by the early French explorers of the area. The plains were created by the glaciers of the Ice Age which, while gouging out areas that became rivers and lakes, generally smoothed and flattened the area's previously rugged topography.

The region can boast of the best agriculture in the country and has traditionally been second only to the Mid-Atlantic states in manufacturing. More corn, wheat, oats, soybeans, hogs, cattle, and dairy products as well as cars, trucks, and farm implements are produced here than in any other area of the nation.

The Allegheny Mountains border the region to the east, and it was this natural barrier that had to be crossed nearly 200 years ago before large-scale settlement could begin. The portion of the region first settled by pioneers is now Ohio. There they found forests, which meant that the land, when cleared, was ideally suited for growing wheat.

Settlers moving west found the plains covered with tall grass. This land was best for raising corn. Today, the corn belt of the North Central Plains covers 250,000 square miles, stretching from the Alleghenies to Kansas, Nebraska, and South Dakota. The westernmost, driest area of the region also is suitable for wheat-growing.

Not only are the North Central Plains ideal for farming, but the flat nature of the land has allowed railways, roads, and pipelines to be built with relative ease. With many rivers (including Illinois' Des Plaines River) to go along with the railways and roads that were eventually constructed, the North Central Plains saw the growth of many cities, as transportation was simple.

Easy transportation meant that cities would be involved in manufacturing. Trading and manufacturing firms had taken root even before the Civil War. Areas of the North Central Plains quickly became known for their leadership in manufacturing a variety of products: steel (Pittsburgh), autos (Detroit), and chemicals (Cleveland). Other cities, such as Chicago and St. Louis, began as transportation hubs, gateways to other areas of the country for the pioneers of the 19th century.

The dairy and timber areas of Wisconsin and Minnesota as well as the oil and natural gas areas of Michigan and Illinois also are vital to the North Central Plains' economic base.

Deer, moose, bear, and fish were abundant in the days of the pioneers but are becoming more and more scarce as urban areas continue to sprawl. They still can be found in the North Woods country of Wisconsin and Minnesota, however.

While manufacturing in the cities of the "Rust Belt" is not as strong as in the past, the region continues to be the nation's most vital agriculturally. A few inches of rainfall per year make all the difference, as to the immediate west in the Great Plains states, farming has always been a more difficult and harsh business.

Fillmore Street

(1024 south)

Fillmore Street is another Near West Side thoroughfare named for a president whom history has nearly forgotten.

Fillmore was the second vice president to succeed to the nation's highest office after the death of the chief executive. In this case, the president was Zachary Taylor, after whom Taylor Street is named. Fillmore, a member of the Whig Party, was the 13th president and served from 1850 to 1853.

Taylor had intended to veto the Compromise of 1850, an amalgam of bills that attempted to appease North and South on the slavery question. Fillmore actively supported the bill and signed it into law. This postponed the Civil War by ten years, but so angered the anti-slavery forces in the North that it made that war inevitable.

Only one other event of great significance occurred under Fillmore's leadership. A naval expedition under the command of Commodore Matthew Perry was sent to Japan, which had been closed to foreign trade for centuries. A treaty was signed between the United States and Japan, thereby moving the latter country into the modern world.

Fillmore wanted the Whig Party's nomination for the presidency in 1852, but his signing of the Fugitive Slave Bill as part of the Compromise of 1850 made him so unpopular in the North that the party chose General Winfield Scott instead. Scott lost the election.

After leaving office in 1853, Fillmore traveled in Europe for a while and came back to receive the nomination of the American "Know-Nothing" Party in 1856. Members of this party, whenever they were asked the party's positions on the issues, replied "I know nothing." Fillmore lost this election, carrying one state.

An early 20th century newspaper columnist, having nothing to report one day, wrote that Fillmore had been the first president to install a bathtub in the White House. Although untrue, this story, ironically, is what Fillmore is best remembered for today. He died in 1874 in Buffalo, New York.

Fillmore Street and nearby Grenshaw Street were the site of a battle over redevelopment in 1996 and 1997. With only a handful of houses left there among a wide expanse of empty lots, a developer wanted the city's help in acquiring the few remaining structures, with the objective being to build 250 new townhouses.

The few neighbors left there were able to fight city hall, however, and they got to keep their homes as the development was built around them.

Flournoy Street

(700 south)

Named for a 1850s Chicago real estate developer, Lafayette M. Flournoy, the street was the home to 23-year-old Lori Roscetti, a Rush-Presbyterian-St. Luke's Medical Student whose brutal murder about a mile south of her residence on Oct. 18, 1986, shocked a tough-as-nails city and was the most gruesome story ever covered by the *Near West/South Gazette.*

A group of neighbors, the Near West Community Committee, began offering scholarships to medical students in 1988 to honor the slain Roscetti.

On a happier note, Flournoy since 1887 has been home to the beautiful Notre Dame de Chicago Church, in whose office complex the *Gazette's* headquarters often has been located.

Originally built for Chicago's French Catholics (where *did* they disappear to, anyway?), Notre Dame was taken over by the Congregation of the Blessed Sacrament in 1917. Their devotional services focusing on the Blessed Sacrament breathed new life into the church, highlighted by Holy Thursday, 1936, when 61,000 people passed through the church. The congregation left Notre Dame in 1992, and the church reverted back to being run by the Chicago Roman Catholic Archdiocese.

Notre Dame even rebounded from a severe fire that occurred on June 7, 1978, to become the centerpiece of the Archdiocese's "Area Planning" process of the early 1990s, which dealt with the problem of six Catholic churches—St. Francis of Assisi, Notre Dame, Holy Family, Holy Trinity, St. Callistus, and Our Lady of Pompeii—operating within a few blocks of each other and how to eliminate that duplication of effort while being sensitive to the needs of each of their different congregations.

The demolition of the parish's 107-year-old school building tugged at the heartstrings of some members of the community, causing some of the bolder to employ the age-old tactic of literally standing in the path of the wrecking equipment to try to stop it. Police arrested two activists, and the building came down.

In 1994, amid objections to boisterous University of Illinois at Chicago students loudly leaving the church hall one night, the police arrested Notre Dame's pastor, Fr. Steve Lanza. The priest had been in bed sleeping only a few minutes before his surprise collar. The charges later were dropped.

Flournoy also was home for many years to community activist Dora Soto, who helped form Concerned Hispanics of the Near West Side to provide opportunities for education, political awareness, and economic mobility for area Hispanics, who for decades have been a vital, although often quiet, part of the Near West Side.

Grenshaw Street

(1132 south)

This side street was named for the Honorable B. Willis Grenshaw, who served as a judge of the Circuit Court for many years in the last century, and then decided to move on to Kentucky.

His judicial skills were tapped by that state's Court of Appeals, and he ended up as chief justice of that branch of the Bluegrass State's judiciary at the time of his death.

A penchant for the bench apparently ran in the family, as his daughter, Arabella, married an Illinois judge, G. Rogers.

Halsted Street

(800 west)

Philadelphia financiers Caleb O. and William H. Halsted helped finance the real estate speculations of Chicago's first mayor, William B. Ogden, for whom Ogden Ave. is named, and so were rewarded with a street named for them as well.

By far the most dominant institution on Halsted in the Near West Side is the University of Illinois at Chicago.

When the University of Illinois decided in 1946 to build a campus in the Chicagoland area, the last place anyone involved in the site selection process dreamed of placing the university complex was on Halsted between Harrison Street and Roosevelt Road.

One of the first sites recommended by the Real Estate Research Corporation, a firm hired by the university to study possible campus locations, was a suburban site west of Chicago known as Miller Meadow. Residential areas such as the Near West Side were ruled out because of the difficulty in moving residents.

The university's board of trustees voted in 1956 to buy the Miller Meadow property, but in doing so came into conflict with the wishes of Mayor Richard J. Daley.

Daley believed that location of the university within the city limits would contribute greatly to the redevelopment of Chicago.

His close political ally, Dan Ryan, was chair of the Cook County Board of Commissioners which, along with the Forest Preserve District, owned Miller Meadow. Both agencies simply refused to sell. University administrators learned a lesson, and cooperated and consulted with the mayor thereafter.

The Central Loop Area Committee, an association of downtown businesses, sought an area near the Loop for the campus' location. Residents and businesses in the Garfield Park area wanted the university built in their neighborhood.

A site had to be chosen before the November 1960 election, because a bond issue to finance the construction of the campus would be on the ballot. The financing would likely be defeated at the polls if the campus' location were still in doubt, as had already happened in the election two years before.

The mayor favored locating the university on railroad terminal land near the Loop, but the railroads were asking too high a price for the property. Park District management was unwilling to sell the Garfield Park land to the university, and Daley, who was just beginning his second term as mayor, had not yet coalesced his power over that agency enough to force it to do so.

The Harrison-Halsted site first came up in 1959 at the suggestion of Phil Doyle, executive director of the city's Land Clearance Commission.

Much of the land already was owned by the city, and properties surrounding the city's holdings could readily be condemned and acquired. The area was close enough to the Loop to please the downtown business leaders. Fifty-five acres on Halsted at Harrison already had been designated as an urban renewal clearance area. Therefore, perhaps most importantly, federal funding would be available under urban renewal programs to pay part of the city's share of the cost of building the university.

However, City Hall had made a commitment to Near West Side residents that urban renewal programs would be used to restore the neighborhood, and that the area owned by the city would be rebuilt for residential use. Many residents had already begun to spend money refurbishing their homes and businesses.

On Sept. 27, 1959, the mayor officially suggested the 55-acre clearance area, and 90 adjacent acres, to the university's board of trustees.

Strangely, there was no protest from the community at first. Many people believed the university would not be built, as several sites had been suggested throughout the years, but groundbreaking was no closer than it had been in 1946. Perhaps it was because the 1st Ward was a loyal Democratic ward, and few believed City Hall would go through with a project that would eliminate the homes of so many voters.

The bond issue for the funding of the proposed construction passed in November 1960, sparking mass protests beginning in 1961.

The demonstrations were led by Florence Scala, a housewife who would be a community activist for the next three decades, and who would go on to establish and run a Taylor Street institution, Florence Restaurant, from 1980 to 1990.

At the time, Scala was a member of the Near West Side Planning Board, a neighborhood organization that had formed in the 1950s to obtain federal funds for rehabilitation of the neighborhood. The board had submitted plans for area improvement, which had been okayed by the federal government.

Because of this, residents were completely surprised by the city's plan.

"The Holy Guardian Angel and St. Francis of Assisi parishes moved fast," Scala said. "They called a neighborhood meeting right away, and sent kids home from school to tell their parents about it."

It was at the meeting that Scala was chosen to become spokesperson for the protests, because she was already knowledgeable in neighborhood planning due to her position on the board, and also because she was one of the few women on it. "Since so much was going to be done during the day, men weren't available," she said. Also, since many of the men were city workers, all felt it prudent for the women to lead the fight.

The protesters held community meetings, petitioned city, state, and federal legislators, and marched and sat-in at City Hall for a full month.

Interestingly enough, none of the supposedly savvy reporters on the City Hall beat paid any attention to the protests at first. In 1961, and especially in Chicago, a grassroots uprising had not been seen in a long time, and reporters did not know what to do with the story. It fell to Georgie Anne Geyer, then a local reporter and later a nationally syndicated columnist, to give the protest publicity.

After Geyer's story appeared, and after Hugh Hill reported the protests on television, "coverage began to snowball," Scala said. The protest marches were ideal for a visual medium like TV. The Near West Side's opposition was the first grassroots campaign against City Hall in Daley's career as mayor. There would be many more.

Although it appeared that most residents of the Near West Side supported the movement, there was some resentment on the part of people living in older houses, who saw the city's plan as an excellent opportunity to sell their properties. "So we made a public statement that people who wished to sell to the city should feel free to do so," Scala said. "But they were in the minority."

It was during the height of the protests that a black-powder bomb was set off at Scala's home, blowing up the porch and staircase. "We never knew if it was done by a disgruntled political worker or homeowner, or by a kook," Scala said.

Despite the bombing, the protests continued and received city-wide support. "We got lots of small contributions from all over the city, and it was very moving to see people who didn't even know us help support us," Scala said.

The protesters initiated a series of legal actions to stop the construction of the campus, but to no avail. Over 100 acres of Near West Side buildings were torn down, and more than 10,000 people left the neighborhood to make way for the University of Illinois-Chicago Circle, which opened in 1965.

The Halsted brothers were well-known for a propensity to foreclose on Chicago property and move people out, and in a strange irony, the street named for them was the main thoroughfare down the most massive moveout of people the city had ever seen.

Despite its troubled birth, the subsequent development of the University of Illinois at Chicago was foreseen by almost no one: due to the quality of its faculty and programs, UIC has become a world-class institution.

In September of 1982, the Medical Center and Chicago Circle campuses of the University of Illinois merged to become the University of Illinois at Chicago. The merger made the relatively new kid on the block the largest institution of higher learning in the Chicago area.

UIC's medical center is listed by *U.S. News & World Report* as among the top four percent in the United States. In recent years, it has ranked seventh in the nation in the number of fellowships awarded to faculty by the National Endowment for the Humanities. Its Great Cities Program is developing a plethora of solutions to a host of problems that affect urban dwellers and urban life. In fiscal 1996, for the first time, UIC's budget was larger than that of the University of Illinois at Urbana.

Many of the inhabitants of today's Near West Side came to the neighborhood as university students or employees, and stayed on as residents. Others like having a university in their backyard. And a significant number can no longer even imagine the Near West Side without the University of Illinois at Chicago. Once derisively called "Harvard on Halsted" by students, in national rankings in several areas the university is hot on the heels of its Ivy League counterparts.

That's a development that once would have seemed as unbelievable as the Halsted brothers turning down a profit on a foreclosure.

Florence Scala, in the meantime, became such a Chicago icon that she was honored in a special exhibit in the Chicago Historical Society in 1989.

Harrison Street

(600 south)

A comparison of former President Ronald Reagan to the president after whom Harrison Street is named reveals many parallels. In fact, the strategies that Reagan employed so successfully in his political campaigns were first created for the 1840 presidential campaign of William Henry Harrison, who would become the nation's ninth chief executive.

Harrison was a major-general in the United States Army during the Indian wars in the early decades of the 19th century, and was the hero of the Battle of Tippecanoe in 1811. After leaving the army, he served as a congressman and senator from Ohio before receiving the Whig Party's nomination for president.

In 1840, Harrison became the first presidential candidate to run an image-oriented, rather than issue-oriented, campaign. Like the campaigns of Ronald Reagan, Harrison's crusade employed patriotic slogans and appeals to traditional American values. To Harrison and his supporters, therefore, must go the credit for creating the first modern political campaign.

The slogan "Tippecanoe and Tyler too" came from this race (John Tyler was Harrison's vice-presidential candidate). Harrison's supporters portrayed him as an average American living in a log cabin (he actually resided in a mansion), and figured that the more they focused the campaign on the candidate's image as a man of the people and the less they focused on real issues, the better Harrison's chance of winning.

The hoopla that the Harrison people injected into the campaign was something new, and as a result, Harrison won the election. He was helped by the unpopularity of Democratic President Martin Van Buren, just as Reagan would be aided by the unpopularity of incumbent Democratic President Jimmy Carter 140 years later.

Harrison, at 68, was the oldest man ever elected president until Ronald Reagan was chosen chief executive at the age of 69 in 1980. Harrison and Reagan both believed in cabinet government, allowing the heads of various departments of the government to exercise much more power than predecessors in those posts had been accustomed to wielding.

A cold Harrison had caught at his inauguration developed into pneumonia, and he became the first president to die in office. His death came exactly one month to the day after he was sworn in as president.

The chief executive's surprise death was not the last odd tragedy to befall the Harrison family. The nation was horrified to learn in the spring of 1878 that grave robbers had dug up the body of the late president's son, Congressman John Scott Harrison, from a cemetery near Cincinnati and had sold it to a medical school for anatomy practice.

Such activities of so-called "resurrectionists" had actually been somewhat commonplace, but the public had been blissfully unaware. Because of the family's prominence, however, the case gained nationwide publicity, and state legislatures across the country passed laws greatly stiffening the penalties for grave robbing. For more than a century, politicians have quite prudently been against grave robbing, which has not been an issue in the public forum.

At least until 1995, when the Illinois State Legislature actually considered a bill that would have crippled burial site preservation laws in the state and eliminated any limitation on property owners' ability to do as they wished with human remains and associated grave artifacts.

In the *Gazette's* first five years of operation, barely a month went by in which an article about National Republic Bank, located on Harrison Street, was not on the front page.

In 1978, the City of Chicago had sold the property on the southwest corner of Harrison and Racine streets to the bank for a drive-up facility, with the stipulation that housing also would be constructed on the site.

By 1983, ground still had not been broken, and the bank was indicted in a drug-money laundering scheme, charged with 34 counts of "failure to report financial transactions as required by law." The bank pled guilty, and its owners sold the institution to a new group of investors the next year.

The new ownership at first wanted to sell the property in question to McDonald's Corp., igniting vehement community opposition. Late in 1985, bank officials withdrew from negotiations with McDonald's and began talking about a sale to developers, prompting the city to take the bank to court to get it to comply with the 1978 agreement or return the property to the city.

What followed was three years of litigation before the bank and the city compromised: the bank would build an office building and drive-up and would not have to construct housing, but would not sell the property off. The building was erected, the bank even proposed to house a local public library branch in it (a community-friendly offer that the city chose not to take up), and the housing expected in 1978 wasn't missed as new units went up all over the neighborhood throughout the 1980s.

Harrison Street also is home to beleaguered Cook County Hospital, which seldom gets the respect it should and often through the years found itself in the political crossfire between Republicans who wanted to cut its already meager funding even more, and Democrats who wanted to tear it down and build a new facility. The Democrats won, and a new facility is under construction. Despite almost a complete dearth of positive publicity, however, Cook County Hospital has actually become world-renowned for its excellence in certain specialties of health care.

Hermitage Street

(1734 west)

Hermitage, like Ashland, is named after a Southern politician's plantation. The Hermitage was owned by the seventh president of the United States, Andrew Jackson, for whom Jackson Boulevard at 300 south is named.

Around the time Tennessee entered the Union in 1796, Jackson bought a 650-acre tract of land 12 miles east of Nashville for $800 and called it the Hermitage. He had been forced to sell a larger plantation because he had been swindled out of much of his money.

From this event grew Jackson's distrust of financiers and complicated financial deals. He always remembered his flight to the Hermitage.

The famous Hermitage mansion was built in 1819, and enlarged in 1831. Going to church on Sunday was no problem; Jackson built one on the property. He and his wife, Rachel, were slaveowners, and the Jacksons' former home cabin was initially used to house the slaves.

Up to 150 slaves worked the plantation, on which cotton, corn, wheat, cows, mules, pigs, and horses were raised. Jackson was one of the first farmers in the area to use a cotton gin, which greatly increased his cotton production; and he loved horses, breeding, training, and racing some of Tennessee's finest.

Jackson was elected president in November 1828, but his wife never made it to Washington, as she died at the Hermitage of heart failure the next month.

After leaving the presidency in 1837, Jackson returned to the Hermitage only to find that his son had mismanaged the plantation in his absence. Jackson, at the age of 70, had to work to get the plantation out of debt, and was successful in doing so. He died in 1845 at the age of 78, and he and Rachel Jackson are buried together at the Hermitage.

Jackson Boulevard

(300 south)

Today's Americans generally agree that the country's elected officials are too closely tied to big-money interests, and that these "leaders" are lacking in the political courage it takes to do what's right if it even remotely endangers their chances of winning the next election.

This was not always the case. Jackson Street/Boulevard, as well as a Near West Side School, Jackson Language Academy, are named for a president of the United States who wasn't afraid to fight the big-money interests and risked losing re-election to destroy the most powerful bank in the nation.

That same Andrew Jackson, after whose home Hermitage Street is named, had been a Tennessee farmer, an army general (the hero of the Battle of New Orleans in the War of 1812), and a U.S. senator when he was elected president in 1828. He ran as a common man from the nation's heartland against the power of the East Coast moneyed elite.

Inauguration day proved that this was no mere campaign tactic, as he threw open the White House to anyone who wanted to come in and join the inauguration party.

Since the presidency of George Washington, the federal government's funds had been deposited in an institution called the Bank of the United States. The bank was not a government agency, but was an independent institution chartered by the government.

With control of the government's funds, the bank was the most powerful financial institution in the nation. Experts believed its policies had caused the depression of 1819, and that its strict credit policies where curtailing the growth of the United States, hitting "the little guy," farmers and small-business owners, particularly hard.

Bank President Nicholas Biddle, with control of the nation's economy in the bank's grasp and knowing Jackson was opposed to the big-money interests, decided to put the president in a tough political spot in 1832. Even though the bank's charter had four years to run, he and the other bank managers demanded rechartering that year, with the implicit threat that the bank might create hard economic times in an election year if the president didn't go along with their wishes.

Jackson observed to Martin Van Buren that, "The bank, Mr. Van Buren, is trying to kill me; but I will kill it," and he vetoed the bank rechartering bill in a strongly worded message.

That made the bank the single issue in the presidential race, and Biddle the bad guy. The issue energized Jackson's campaign, although the bank's power to strangle the nation's economy at the whim of a few money men accountable to no one was by no means clear to all the voters.

Although Jackson was reelected, enough people voted against him because of the bank issue that he won by a smaller majority in his second election than in his first, which had never happened to a president, before or since. Jackson staked his reelection on doing what was right, and many people did not understand this and voted against him.

The next year, Jackson started removing the government's money from the bank. Purely in retaliation, the bank cut back credit drastically and interest rates rose from six to 15 percent. A recession resulted, which only proved that Jackson had been right. Any independent institution that could create a recession merely out of anger was too powerful to remain in existence.

And Jackson, called an "economic illiterate" by opponents, so wisely managed the government's funds in his second term that the budget not only balanced, but had a surplus of $28 million by 1835.

The economic battles of this era had effects even down to the presidential election of 1996.

The Federal Reserve's trimming of the interest rate charged for overnight loans between banks by 0.25 percent in July of 1995 had many economic experts wondering why the Fed even bothered. Typical was the reaction of economist Ken Goldstein of the New York-based research group The Conference Board, who told the *Chicago Sun-Times* that the rate decline "is so small that it makes you scratch your head. What are they telling us?"

When viewed through the prism of presidential politics, however, which even 16 months before the election already was driving everything in Washington, the decision was a wise one. What the Fed and Fed Chairman Alan Greenspan were telling everyone is that they would not be "Biddleized."

Greenspan and the Fed had already been accused of meddling in 1996 presidential politics via their six increases in short-term interest rates in 1994. As Peter Klenow, assistant professor of business economics at the University of Chicago Graduate School of Business pointed out in *GSB*

Chicago magazine, "We knew the Fed was going to raise rates. But over the last 20 years [the Fed] has waited until there were signs of inflation actually rising before raising rates." In 1994, Klenow said, "they weren't going to wait." Such atypical actions brought charges that the Fed was trying to slow down an economic expansion that could only help the reelection possibilities of President Bill Clinton.

Clinton, who has read and studied biographies of all the presidents, might have taken the chapter on the bank issue from Jackson's history as his 1996 re-election guide. But Alan Greenspan is no Nicholas Biddle. The Fed's rate trim served notice on Bill Clinton that he'd have to find another key issue on which to base his campaign in 1996.

It was obvious that President Clinton had examined the chapter on achieving a monetary surplus in Jackson's bio, however, as he came out for a balanced budget during the battle with Congress over the deficit in late 1995 and early 1996.

A Near West Side public school at the corner of Harrison and Loomis streets, Jackson Language Academy, also is named for the late President Jackson. The school in its previous location at 820 S. Carpenter was the focus of one of the goofier scandals covered by the *Near West/South Gazette.* In 1990, two needed classrooms were renovated into administrative offices based on an assessment by a consultant hired by the Board of Education. The consultant figured the school didn't require the classrooms—because he had visited Jackson in the *summer,* when few students were around.

All in all, a fine Chicago example of your tax dollars at work.

Mercy Home for Boys and Girls at 1140 W. Jackson has been an area fixture for more than 110 years, and was a major cause of the revitalization of the area west of the loop. Father James Close, president of Mercy Home, gathered area residents and property owners at his facility beginning in 1990 in an attempt to upgrade a very dangerous area. They formed an organization they called "West Loop Gate" (19th century urban planner Daniel Burnham envisioned the area as the "gateway" to the city), and so began the comeback of what by the end of the decade became one of the city's most desirable neighborhoods.

Farther west, the 1500 block of west Jackson was designated a Chicago landmark in order to save the collection of 19th century townhouses there. The plan worked, and the block now is one of the more desirable to live on in the area.

Jefferson Street

(600 west)

At one particularly noteworthy White House dinner in the early 1960s, President John F. Kennedy looked around the room and saw some of the most brilliant scholars in the world and government officials of the highest rank and accomplishment.

"This," said Kennedy, "is the most impressive assemblage of intellect ever at a White House dinner. Except, of course, for when Thomas Jefferson dined here alone."

Jefferson Street is named for the man who was not only the third president of the United States, but one of the most accomplished and brilliant men who ever lived. Jefferson not only was a statesman; he was a philosopher, architect, inventor, linguist, and agricultural engineer. He touches Americans' lives every day, in areas as broad as the security of our freedoms, to items as simple as the chairs on which we sit.

Jefferson was the foremost thinker and writer among the founders of this country. He introduced a radical idea into the world: that the rich and powerful did not have a right to rule the mass of people, but that the people themselves should make the laws. He was the author of the Declaration of Independence, which articulated this philosophy and has served as the blueprint for opposition to elitist governments ever since.

After serving in the Continental Congress that declared the United States' independence, Jefferson was elected Governor of Virginia and wrote four laws that changed U.S. society forever.

One abolished the law of entails, which forbade people from selling their own property and required them to leave it to their descendants. A second abolished primogeniture, which required people to bequeath all their property to the eldest son, leaving nothing for other relatives. A third established religious freedom, and a fourth created free education.

Since Virginia was at that time one of the most powerful states, once it passed these laws other states and the United States followed suit, providing Americans with freedoms they had never before known.

Jefferson was the first Secretary of State, serving in President George Washington's cabinet. He was the first presidential candidate to lose an election (to John Adams; Washington had run unopposed), the first defeated presidential candidate to come back to win the presidency in a later election, and the first candidate to beat an incumbent president.

He always felt that his defeat of Adams for the presidency in 1800 had saved democracy, as he believed that Adams and Secretary of the Treasury Alexander Hamilton were establishing an elitist government.

It was Jefferson who made the decision to double the size of the country by purchasing from France the Louisiana Territory, an area that stretched from the Mississippi River to the Rocky Mountains and from what today are the continental United States' northern and southern borders.

The third president was perhaps the strongest defender of freedom of the press ever to occupy the presidency. "If I had to choose between government without newspapers, or newspapers without government, I should not hesitate to choose the latter," he said.

Jefferson's life-long devotion to and articulation of the philosophies of religious freedom, freedom of speech, and intellectualism have made him a hero to progressives all over the world.

His house, Monticello, which he designed with practicality and with countless labor-saving devices, is depicted on the back of the nickel, which bears his likeness on the front. He invented the mechanically operated double-door (as seen today on busses and el trains), the folding chair, and the swivel chair.

After some years of animosity resulting from the 1800 election, Jefferson and Adams late in life again became good friends, as they had been before the election. Both died on July 4, 1826, the 50th Fourth of July in American history. Not knowing of each other's deaths, Jefferson uttered the last words "And Adams lives," while Adams' last words were, "And Jefferson lives."

On his tombstone, Jefferson wanted listed what he considered to be the greatest accomplishments of his life: the Declaration of Independence, the Virginia Statute of Religious Freedom, and the establishment of the University of Virginia. Nowhere does it mention that he was president of the United States.

Laflin Street

(1500 west)

In the 19th century, Chicago business leaders often were quite generous when asked to contribute money to charitable causes. Matthew Laflin, after whom Laflin Street is named, was one of Chicago's early businessmen/philanthropists.

Laflin came to Chicago in 1838. His first business venture was in the manufacture of gunpowder, and he quickly found a market for his product during the construction of the Illinois and Michigan Canal, which began at Ashland Avenue and the south branch of the Chicago River.

With the money he made in the gunpowder business, Laflin began buying large tracts of real estate and eventually became a rich man. He then built the Bull's Head Hotel, a resort for men in the cattle business. Located at Ogden Avenue and Madison Street, the hotel was constructed complete with cattle pens, which the hotel's residents used as shelter for their livestock while staying at the inn. After its heyday, the hotel was used as an asylum for alcoholics before being torn down.

In 1892, Laflin made a lasting contribution to Chicagoans by donating $75,000 toward the building of a structure to house the Chicago Academy of Sciences, a scholarly society formed to promote the scientific investigation of natural history. As a result of Laflin's gift, the Academy of Sciences was granted a plot of land at 2001 N. Clark Street in Lincoln Park for its building; the Lincoln Park Board of Commissioners then donated $25,000 in public funds to assure adequate financing for the project.

The building opened as the Matthew Laflin Memorial on October 31, 1894, and housed the academy until it moved to North Pier, at 435 E. Illinois, on July 22, 1995. The Matthew Laflin Memorial then reverted to the Chicago Park District, which rehabbed it in 1996 for the Lincoln Park Zoo's administrative offices. The academy is then moved into a new building.

Laflin Street was the site of the 1994 shooting of popular Chicago Blackhawks singer and announcer Wayne Messmer. Messmer recovered to sing again—then was promptly given his pink slip by Blackhawks management.

Lexington Street

(732 south)

Lexington Street is named for the battle of Lexington and Concord, the first military conflict of the Revolutionary War.

Lexington and Concord are small towns located about 12 miles northwest of Boston in Massachusetts. In the early morning hours of April 19, 1775, at Lexington, 70 colonial militiamen met 800 British soldiers, who were attempting to capture a cache of American ammunition stored at Concord. The colonists were forewarned that the British were coming by the famous midnight ride of Paul Revere.

Captain John Parker, who commanded the colonists, refused to disburse his men when ordered to do so by Major John Pitcairn, the British commander, so the British opened fire. Eight Americans were killed at Lexington before the remaining colonial troops retreated to Concord.

At Concord, the militia numbered about 200, and they fought so well that the British, who suffered several casualties, were forced to try to retreat to Boston. In the course of their retreat, they were met by American ambushes all the way. British reinforcements joined the retreating troops back at Lexington, but the colonists had the upper hand in the battle and completely routed the Redcoats, killing 300 of them.

This victorious battle thrilled and fortified Americans throughout the 13 colonies, assuring them that their troops could beat the British in a military conflict.

A boulder, inscribed with Captain Parker's order to the militiamen to stand their ground, marks the battle line at Lexington. A monument was erected there in 1799 to commemorate the eight Americans who lost their lives in the battle of Lexington.

Among the other historical sites of Lexington are the Hancock-Clarke House, where Sam Adams and John Hancock were warned by Paul Revere of the British march; the Buckman Tavern, where the colonials met before the battle; and the Munroe Tavern, which the British used as a hospital during the conflict. All are now museums.

Lexington is one of the streets that borders Victor Arrigo Park, known in the neighborhood as "Peanut Park." The neighborhood, which generally favors an "active" Arrigo Park where young and old can participate in sport, has since the 1960s battled off-and-on with the Chicago Park District and several community leaders, who have wanted to turn the park into a "passive" park with trees, flowers, and landscapes—and no recreational facilities.

A compromise was reached in 1986 that set aside areas of the park for both purposes.

Lexington also is the site of Our Lady of Pompeii, a Roman Catholic Church that provided that "old-time religion" through the traditionalist Scalabrinian Order that ran it and nearby St. Callistus Parish (on Bowler Street). The order announced its departure from the two parishes in 1992, and Pompeii now is a shrine.

Liberty Street

(1344 south)

In 1915, Philadelphia's Liberty Bell traveled from the City of Brotherly Love to San Francisco for the Panama-Pacific Exposition, and stopped in the City of Big Shoulders along the way. Liberty Street was named for this quintessential American symbol.

Pennsylvania ordered the bell for its state house in Philadelphia in 1752, which was a little more than 50 years after the state's founder, William Penn, issued the Charter of Priviledges that granted liberties to the state's citizens. The legislators were inspired by a Bible verse, Leviticus 25:10, which reads, "And ye shall hallow the fiftieth year, and proclaim liberty throughout all the land."

The first time the bell was rung, it cracked. Since it had been ordered from England, it was not exactly easy to send it back, so it was recast.

Over the years, the bell has rung in many events in the annals of liberty: the convening of the assemblies that sent Benjamin Franklin to England in 1757 and 1764 to present the colonies' grievances, as well as one that called for the repeal of tea taxes in 1771; the announcement of the Battle of Lexington and Concord in 1775; the first public reading of the Declaration of Independence in 1776; the two inaugurations of President John Adams, and more.

An 1839 poem featured the first documented use of the term "Liberty Bell."

In 1846, while being rung to celebrate George Washington's birthday, the bell cracked again, and remains so to this day.

Although it is one of the most famous symbols of the nation, its ownership actually is in question. It seems that when Pennsylvania decided to rebuild the state house in the early 19th century, it decided to replace the bell as well. As part of the deal for his providing a replacement, bellcaster John Wilbank was supposed to haul the Liberty Bell away. He never did, and after litigation a court ruled that the City of Philadelphia would keep the bell on loan from the Wilbank family. In 1915, the family stipulated that the city could continue to keep it so long as it hung in Independence Hall.

To celebrate the bicentennial in 1976, the bell was moved to a National Park Service pavilion across the street. An heir of Wilbank's later tried to claim it, threatening to melt it down and use its metal for rings that he would put up for sale.

He failed, and the bell remains in the pavilion, with both Philadelphia and Wilbank's heirs claiming ownership.

Eighteenth century concepts of liberty inspired the formation of a 20th and 21st century political party, the Libertarian Party, which has been particularly active in the area. Local resident Maggie Kohls ran for the State Senate and for Congress under the Libertarian Party banner, and William Passmore sought a Congressional seat in the area twice—once after winning a rare contested Libertarian primary.

Loomis Street

(1400 west)

Chicago's four financial trading exchanges are a vital economic asset to the international economy. And without Horatio G. Loomis, after whom Loomis Street is named, these financial powerhouses might not have been created.

Loomis was a native of Vermont who came to Chicago as a pioneer settler in 1834. A grocer by trade, Loomis also was an entrepreneur who became involved in many business fields, including commodities trading.

Chicago, being the transportation hub of the nation's breadbasket, was the most logical location for the agricultural commodities futures trading business.

Loomis was one of the organizers of the Chicago Board of Trade in 1848. Initially, the CBOT dealt only in futures contracts for agricultural products. Subsequently, it began dealing in precious metals.

The CBOT later developed into a more broad-based futures exchange that cleared and settled trades and offered standardized contracts. Today, it deals primarily in financial products, such as treasury notes, municipal bonds, and stocks.

In futures trading, investors bid on products based on what they think the price of the product will be at a later date. The products themselves usually do not even change hands, as money is gained or lost solely on the sales of futures contracts.

The CBOT was so successful that other futures exchanges were started in Chicago: the Chicago Mercantile Exchange, the Midwest Stock Exchange, and the Chicago Board Options Exchange.

Today, the four exchanges directly provide 33,000 jobs, as well as more than 110,000 ancillary jobs. Nearly $1 billion is pumped into the local economy by the exchanges' dealings. And, the four exchanges' members constitute the largest concentration of futures and options trades in the world.

Loomis died in 1900. Thanks to him and his contemporaries, the actions of Chicago traders daily directly influence the actions of financiers in New York, London, Tokyo, and the rest of the world.

The first lead article ever published in the *Near West/South Gazette* concerned Loomis Street. The *Gazette's* inaugural issue in 1983 reported that community members had hit the streets to protest the proposed construction of 200 units of subsidized public housing in an area of land known as Academy Square bounded by Loomis, Jackson, Throop, and Van Buren Streets.

With approximately 9,000 subsidized units already located in the area, residents were concerned that another 200 would push the percentage of subsidized housing in the area above 18 percent, which exceeded even the U.S. Department of Housing and Urban Development's maximum allowable amount of 15 percent.

As always, political clout was involved as the sellers and developers of the property were big contributors to Mayor Jane Byrne's political fund.

Community opponents not only picketed, but endeavored to have an economic impact as many closed accounts in the two banks that were the developers.

The Academy Square development was built anyway, but the community came out all right. A decade of gentrification created more private housing, decreasing the percentage of subsidized residences. Byrne lost the mayoralty that year, and has never won an election since.

Loomis Street also is the site of the girls' programs for Midtown Center, located at 718 south (boys programs operate at another facility outside the neighborhood). There is something about Midtown and its parallel facility, the Metro Achievement Program (two special-education centers for junior-high aged students) that attracted the attention of presidents of the United States in 1986 when the Near West Side facility offered coed programs. In May of that year, the *Gazette* reported that President Ronald Reagan recognized the programs for the "tremendous progress" they were making in preparing youngsters for entrance to high school, college, and careers. In July of that same year, former President Jimmy Carter visited Midtown and Metro for a discussion with the students on helping others.

Carter was in town through Habitat for Humanity International, which works to build homes for poor people worldwide. That year's annual Jimmy Carter Work Project constructed homes on the nearby West Side. Instead of staying at a fancy downtown hotel, Carter spent his nights right in the neighborhood.

The *Near West/South Gazette* early on contributed to the reassessment and renaissance of Jimmy Carter through writing on the editorial page about the good works he performs.

The former president heads the Carter Center of Atlanta's Emory University. The center works as an international service organization. Its projects, in which Carter is personally involved, include disease eradication, promotion of human rights, resolution of international conflicts, and alleviation of hunger.

At a question-and-answer session this reporter covered, Carter said he and the center do not take on projects that anyone else can handle. In a sense, he specializes in "lost causes," which become winnable causes with his group's help. For example, he and his group are working to wipe out the disease "Guinea Worm," an insidious parasite that affects Third World natives. Experts agree that this effort will be successful, but it wouldn't have happened at all without the Carter Center.

There are no international mechanisms for resolving disputes between fighting factions within countries, such as civil wars, so Carter and the center have stepped into this breach, again with success. Even the elder President George Bush gave Carter full credit for facilitating a non-violent transition from the Sandinistas to their opponents in Nicaragua. And of course, Carter led peace missions to Haiti and North Korea for President Bill Clinton.

Loomis Street also borders the 911 center, the hub for all of Chicago's police and fire communications.

On Jan. 29, 1996, the street was the site of a tragedy as Don C. Piemonte was killed when his car crashed into an illegally parked truck trailer at approximately 2401 S. Loomis. Piemonte who, along with his wife, Mary Ann, owned and operated University Village Day Care and Pre-School on Taylor Street, was one of the area's best-loved residents.

"Donnie was young, but he believed in old-fashioned values," said former 1st Ward Alderman Ted Mazola. "He was a man of his word and you always knew where he stood."

"I *know* the gates to Heaven opened when Donnie knocked," said Mark Valentino, ending the eulogy at Piemonte's funeral.

Lytle Street

(1235 west)

Lytle is one of several Chicago streets named for Civil War heroes.

The second regiment organized by the Chicago Board of Trade, the 88th Illinois Infantry was mustered into the army in August, 1862. That infantry, and especially its First Brigade, constantly found itself in the midst of some of the Civil War's bloodiest battles (see Bell Street listing).

With the public in a state of near panic due to Confederate General Braxton Bragg's invasion of Kentucky, the 88th Illinois was quickly dispatched to the front. There, it was thrown into two bloody major battles: the battle of Perryville and, three months later, the battle of Murfreesboro, also known as the battle of Stone River. At Stone River, the First Brigade's commander, General Sill, was killed leading a charge.

After two interim commanders, General William H. Lytle of Chicago was assigned command of the First Brigade. Lytle, a writer, had achieved some renown with his book *Antony and Cleopatra.*

The 88th Illinois, as part of the Army of the Cumberland, spent the summer of 1863 marching through Tennessee, Alabama, and Georgia.

In September 1863, the Army of the Cumberland fought a battle near Crawfish Springs in northern Georgia (just south of Chattanooga, Tenn.). In this, the battle of Chickamauga (so named for the river flowing near the site), Lytle's troops had just taken position when the forces were fiercely assaulted by Confederates. The 88th fought bravely for half an hour against vastly superior numbers.

Finally, subjected to both frontal and flank fire, the troops were compelled to retreat. It was at this point that Lytle was fatally shot.

In the battle of Chickamauga, the 88th lost one-third of the men who participated in the fight—a total of about 100 killed.

The 88th left Chicago in 1862 with 900 men, and it returned in 1865 with only 209. Its casualties, besides occurring at Perryville, Stone River, and Chickamauga, also were numbered at Mission Ridge, Resaca, Peach Tree Creek, and Franklin—major battles all. The infantry's flag, at the end a bunch of shreds, was returned to the Board of Trade, which had originally presented it.

Lytle Street was the home of one of the most influential figures in baseball history: Charles A. Comiskey.

Born Aug. 15, 1859, he was the third of the eight children of John and Annie Comiskey. Their home was on Lytle between Taylor and 12th (now Roosevelt Road), and they were members of Holy Family Parish. "Honest John" was the political boss of the ward, serving as an alderman from 1859 to 1863 and again from 1867 to 1870. During the Civil War, he organized a unit of the militia made up of his Near West Side neighbors and other immigrants.

"Honest John" would have liked his son to become a businessman or a plumber, but Charles liked playing baseball. Over the objections of his father, he joined a local semipro team. Charles attended St. Ignatius College at Holy Family, the forerunner of Loyola University, and played ball there as well.

His father then sent Charles to St. Mary's College in Kansas, where, John hoped, Charles would not have the opportunity to play ball. Instead, Charles there met a man named Ted Sullivan, who owned a ballclub in Milwaukee. Sullivan signed him, and Comiskey received his first paycheck for taking the field. He couldn't believe that someone would pay someone else to play baseball, a sentiment he would unfortunately continue to hold as an owner later.

In 1882, Sullivan used his influence to get Comiskey a spot on the St. Louis Browns' roster as first baseman and manager. The Browns were in the American Association, which was then the second major league.

In 1885, the Browns won their league's pennant, and met the National League champions, the Cubs (then called the White Stockings) in the World Series. On Oct. 14, 1885, Comiskey returned to the Near West Side as a professional as the series opened in the N.L. champs' park. It was a bitter series, which ended in a tie after one game was called due to darkness.

The next year both teams again copped their leagues' pennants, and Comiskey returned to the old neighborhood to win the world championship. Comiskey batted .292 in each series, and on defense played off of the first-base bag, a radical style of fielding at the time.

In 1890, many players left both major leagues to form a third major loop, the Players' League. Comiskey was one of them, because he wanted to manage and play in Chicago. So that year, he ran the Chicago Pirates, who played in a rickety wooden ballpark at 35th Street and Shields Avenue, where the original Comiskey Park would later stand from 1910 to 1990.

The league folded after that year, so the Lytle Street native went back to St. Louis for one year and then signed with the N.L.'s Cincinnati Reds. It was in Cincinnati that he met Ban Johnson, a disgruntled sportswriter, and the two of them hatched the idea of forming a new league.

Johnson created the circuit as the triple-A level Western League, and Comiskey bought the Sioux City, Iowa, franchise, which won the league's first pennant. Low attendance caused him to move the team to St. Paul, Minn. In 1900, he uprooted the club again, heading back to Chicago to take the old Cubs' team name, the White Stockings or "White Sox." The squad played at 39th Street and Wentworth Avenue.

In 1901, the league changed its name from Western to American and declared itself major. The White Sox won the first A.L. pennant. They were champs again in 1906, and that year the "Hitless Wonder" White Sox beat the highly favored Cubs in the World Series. Comiskey's Sox next won in 1917, beating the New York Giants in the series.

By that time, they were playing in Comiskey Park. It was in the building of this facility that Comiskey's reputation for being tight with a dollar was established. The architect, Zachary Taylor Davis, came up with plans for building a stadium without posts, which would have made Comiskey Park the first such facility in the country, but when Comiskey learned it would cost $100,000 more, he built a standard park instead. Today, $100,000 wouldn't even come close to paying Frank Thomas' monthly salary.

It has been said that it was the low salaries Comiskey paid that were responsible for several players being susceptible enough to take bribes to throw the 1919 World Series to Cincinnati. The White Sox team, which looked poised for a dynasty, was destroyed as Commissioner Kenesaw Mountain Landis banned eight players from the 1919 squad from baseball forever.

Comiskey was devastated by the scandal, and he and his team never recovered.

Although frugal in business, Comiskey was generous in charity. He frequently opened his ballparks for benefits for nuns and orphans.

The "Old Roman," as Charles Comiskey was called, died in 1931. In terms of accomplishment, he had come a long way from the days when his father hoped he would be a laborer fixing plumbing on Lytle Street.

Madison Street

(dividing line between north and south)

Madison Street shoots straight as an arrow from downtown out to the suburbs and beyond. That direct thoroughfare is in stark contrast to the streets of Washington, DC, which splay out from the White House like wagon spokes from the hub of a wheel.

They were designed that way on purpose to give the president of the United States a choice of escape routes in case the capital were being invaded. Only one president has had to leave Washington under such circumstances—James Madison, the fifth president of the United States.

Like many of the founders of the nation, Madison had already achieved greatness even before ascending to the nation's highest office. As a delegate to the Constitutional Convention, Madison wrote most of what would become the United States Constitution, and so is considered its originator.

At five feet, six inches, Madison was the country's shortest president—and the lightest, too, weighing just over 100 pounds. Writer Washington Irving called him a "withered little apple," but Madison's small physical stature proved to be no barrier in his winning the heart of the vivacious and popular Dolley Todd, whom he later married. Dolley Madison was the most celebrated and popular first lady until Jacqueline Kennedy captured the public's affection 150 years later.

In the War of 1812, the Madisons were forced to flee what was then called the "President's Mansion" during an 1814 British invasion. The British captured the mansion, gobbled up the food they found there, and tried to burn the place to the ground.

Although they were unsuccessful, the exterior was so scorched that during rehabbing of the building after the war, it was painted white to cover up the burn marks. The public began calling the mansion the "White House," and it has been so designated ever since.

There were no mansions on Madison Street in Chicago, as for much of its existence it was home to skid row. In fact, more than 80 years ago the West Central Association (WCA) was formed by area businesspeople to fight the area's wino image.

The first improvement on the street in many decades came in 1968 when a Holiday Inn was constructed on Madison at Halsted. The hotel was expected to be the opening to full redevelopment of the area, but a subsequent Nixon-era recession kept the hotel the only new construction in the skid row area for many years. Owner Frank J. Caputo and his associates had to work especially hard to make a go of it. He eventually left the hotel, but bought it back in 1984 and turned it into a Quality Inn.

The area suffered another reversal in 1976-77 when the garment trades that lined the street moved away. The community was then faced with empty properties, but under the leadership of Executive Director Bob Wiggs, the WCA promoted adaptive reuse of the structures into residential, office, and small business facilities.

The 1980s and 1990s saw an invasion of gentrification that ejected the city's down-and-outers as effectively as the British chased away President Madison.

Presidential Towers at 555 W. Madison was the first gentrified development. It also was supposed to provide a home for the skid row denizens whose single resident occupancy facilities were being replaced, but that was never a priority of the development and court battles ensued for years.

For most of this century, parents would wag a finger at ne'er-do-well offspring and tell them if they didn't watch out, they would end up on Madison Street. With townhouses worth hundreds of thousands of dollars now lining the thoroughfare, that threat has instead become a fond wish.

Marshfield Street

(1634 west)

Some Chicago street names are self-explanatory. The name Marshfield does not honor a person or a place, but describes the topographic condition of early Chicago: a marsh.

Chicago was called "The Mudhole of the Prairies" in the middle of the 19th century. The land, being flat and low (only two feet above the Chicago River on the average), barely drained at all.

The city grew up fast after its incorporation in 1833, but sanitation and ease of transport were seldom considered during early building. By 1848, Chicago still had no sewers, no sidewalks (save for a few planks haphazardly strewn about), and no paved streets. Mud was to be found everywhere.

A mud hole deeper than usual would be marked by a sign reading, "No bottom here, the shortest route to China." Whenever a fire occurred it usually burned uncontrollably, because fire engines got stuck in the muddy streets, as firemen helplessly watched the blazes burn.

The little water that did flow out of the city took sewage with it and flowed into Lake Michigan, which also, of course, was the source of Chicago's drinking water. Epidemics of cholera, typhoid, and other diseases therefore were common.

After 1,424 Chicagoans died in a cholera epidemic in 1854, the city council decided to elevate the streets. Landfill placement resulted in the streets being raised up to 12 feet. This is why in older areas of the city, including certain parts of the Near West Side, homes still exist with their first floors below street level.

That same year, it was proved that even major buildings could be lifted out of the mud, as the Tremont Hotel was placed on jacks and lifted eight feet "without disturbing a guest or cracking a cup." Thereafter, several thousand acres were lifted up to five feet, and for a while, predominantly flat Chicago more resembled San Francisco, as some owners raised their properties while others did not.

In 1889, in the wake of another epidemic, the Chicago Sanitary District (now the Metropolitan Water Reclamation District) was created, and the commission decided to reverse the current of the Chicago River so it would flow away from Lake Michigan. This, coupled with the raising of the land, eliminated marshes from Chicago.

The street Marshfield was named in 1869 by Henry D. Gilpin, an Englishman who made his money in Chicago as a landowner and subdivider. He also had been responsible for naming Arthington Street (900 south) ten years earlier after his home town of Arthington, England. Both streets first appeared in a subdivision he owned.

Maxwell Street

(1300 south)

Carl Sandburg wrote poetry about it. William Jennings Bryan gave a speech to a massive crowd on it. Bandleader Benny Goodman and U.S. Supreme Court Justice Arthur Goldberg grew up on it. John Belushi and Dan Aykroyd did a movie on it. Muddy Waters played the blues on it. Bluesmen Papa Charlie Jackson and Robert Nighthawk sang about it. Morrie Mages started his business empire on it.

Maxwell has been Chicago's "Street of Dreams." "It is," says co-director of the 1993 Maxwell Street Market Colloquium Lori Grove, "a cultural phenomenon unlike anywhere else." Grove also is a member of the board of the Maxwell Street Historic Preservation Coalition, created in 1998 in an effort to preserve what remained of the buildings of Maxwell Street.

Shown as a platted street as early as 1849, Maxwell Street originally stretched west from the South Branch of the Chicago River to Blue Island Avenue. Maxwell initially served as a residential street composed of frame cottages built to accommodate the flood of Irish and German immigrants coming into Chicago with the introduction of the railroads in the city in the 1850s.

After the Chicago Fire in 1871, which spread north and east from Chicago's Near West Side, Maxwell Street remained unscathed. Chicagoans flooded the area to gain housing and re-establish businesses.

"The intersection near Maxwell at Jefferson Street particularly catered to the incoming masses as street peddling and street-side stands thrived along Jefferson's north-south streetcar line," Grove said. "This eventually pushed the peddling activity west along Maxwell Street, which was much wider than neighboring streets."

Eastern European Jews, who displaced the Irish and Germans in the 1870s and 1880s, capitalized on the market activity by opening stores in front of their frame houses along the street. Some started calling the area "Jewtown," a moniker used by some older Chicagoans to this day.

Due to health and social improvement movements that prompted housing reform in Chicago in the 1880s and 1890s, most of Maxwell Street's overcrowded frame dwellings were replaced by two- and three-story brick storefronts that perpetuated the market activity. At the turn of the century, the Maxwell Street neighborhood was the most crowded in Chicago, and bore a great resemblance to New York City's Lower East Side.

In 1912, as part of an effort to control street peddling within certain areas of the city, the city government recognized Maxwell Street's market as the city's official open-air market. "Hastily built street sheds, which extended the function of the storefronts and lined the curbs for multiple blocks, uniquely characterized the Maxwell Street Market until nearly the end of the 20th century," Grove noted.

The year 1913 saw the name of the street changed to 13th Place, but then immediately changed back to Maxwell by a unanimous, raucous vote within the City Council. By the next decade, the area was rated the third highest in sales in the city. Stores like S.S. Kresge and Woolworth's were built right around the corner from Maxwell Street, and prominent Jewish architects were hired by local merchants to design new stores and to provide facelifts for storefront facades.

Maxwell Street's importance to the history of Jewish-American architecture is little known, but Grove's research has discovered that whenever Maxwell Street was improved, Jewish-American architects led the way. Alexander Levy, Alfred Alschuler, Henry and George Dubin, Henry Leopold Newhouse, Maurice Spitzer, Abraham Eisenberg, and David Saul Klafter all were great Jewish-American architects who left their mark on the Maxwell Street area.

The early influence of art deco could be seen on Maxwell at Halsted, replacing the appearance of the mixed-use storefront with completely commercial buildings. At the same time, the Jewish merchants were moving their residences further west but keeping their businesses and properties in the Maxwell Street neighborhood.

The 1920s also saw "the influx of Hispanic and African American populations in a continuum of ethnic, residential transition," Grove said. But entrepreneurial business operators such as Morrie Mages, who operated out of several storefronts on Maxwell Street, and Bernard Abrams, who ran a radio store at 831 W. Maxwell, where he recorded some of Chicago's notable blues musicians, earned their livelihoods on Maxwell Street.

Maxwell Street's reputation as a place for "street haggling" where "bargains could be found" continued to escalate so uncontrollably during the 1930s that in 1939 the Maxwell Street Merchants Association was created. Part of the larger Maxwell Street Civic Improvement Project, the association attempted to clean up and standardize appearances of storefronts and street stands on Maxwell Street, and generally organize and improve merchant operations in the Maxwell Street shopping district.

Spearheaded by business expert and New Yorker Ira Wolfe, the Merchants Association was dedicated to "the welfare of business and property owners alike." Headquartered at 722 W. Maxwell in the street's only manufacturing facility (built in 1899 to house Nabisco's first operations in Chicago), the association was short-lived.

"Electrified blues" was born on Maxwell Street in the 1940s, as street musicians literally plugged into electricity inside the stores and residences along the street. That decade saw a decline in residential income levels in the area, and by the 1950s Maxwell became targeted by the City of Chicago for urban renewal.

In 1956, the entire section of Maxwell Street east of the 700 block was cleared for construction of the Dan Ryan Expressway, and in the 1980s, the University of Illinois at Chicago published its "40-Year Plan" that included expansion of its east campus South of Roosevelt Road.

Due to UIC's pending expansion, the City of Chicago relocated the Maxwell Street Market to Canal Street in 1994, and immediately following, all but one of the remaining blocks of Maxwell Street west of Halsted were cleared, with the exception of the 7th District Police Station at 949 W. Maxwell, known nationwide to fans of the *Hill Street Blues* television show. The building was listed on the National Register of Historic Places in 1996, and now serves as the headquarters for the UIC police.

"Today, Maxwell Street west of Halsted is a conglomeration of university athletic fields and housing developments, with no indication that a century-old street market lay beneath the pavement," Grove said.

The University of Illinois at Chicago and City of Chicago's plan to expand the university and develop housing in the old Maxwell Street Market area will change the face of the area once more—just as the faces of the many ethnic groups whose Grove's research showed served as vendors, musicians, and shoppers on Maxwell Street, changed the face of the Near West Side, the city, the nation, and the world forever.

Maxwell Street, like Dr. Philip Maxwell, for whom it is named, played a huge role in the city's history. (Dr. Maxwell himself literally also was huge. An early Chicago history describes him as "Falstaffian in his abdominal rotundity.")

64

Born in Vermont in 1799, Maxwell moved to New York State where he became a doctor and politician, being elected to the state legislature. He also was a physician for the U.S. Army, where he served with General Zachary Taylor, for whom Taylor Street is named. A military transfer brought him to Chicago, which he decided to make his home after resigning from the service. His doctor's office was at the corner of Clark and Lake streets. Known for his jolly demeanor, the physician died in 1859 in Lake Geneva, Wisconsin, where he had a second residence.

May Street

(1134 west)

Ah, Chicago—where government works in strange ways.

When members of the Chicago City Council named the street at 1134 west after the ship *Mayflower,* they did not call it that name exactly; they dubbed it May. It seems that May was Mayor James Curtiss' daughter's name, and the aldermen figured they would honor her as well.

The *Mayflower* was the ship on which the Pilgrims sailed from England in 1620 to establish the first permanent northern English colony in what would become the United States. (Jamestown had been established in the South, in Virginia in 1607.)

The 101 Pilgrims included 35 members of the radical Puritan English Separatist Church, who originated the idea for the voyage. The rest of the group consisted of persons hired by the London stock company that financed the trip.

Previously a wine ship, the *Mayflower,* along with the *Speedwell,* set sail for America from Southampton, England, on Aug. 15, 1620. However, the duo had to return because the *Speedwell* was sinking. After repairs, the ships re-embarked, but had to turn around again as the *Speedwell* still leaked.

With this turn of events, many passengers on both ships got disgusted and gave up. The remainder all left together on the *Mayflower,* which began its solo voyage on Sept. 16.

The *Mayflower* was aimed to reach the mouth of the Hudson River (present-day New York City), but buffeted by high seas and bad weather, did not make it, dropping anchor in Massachusetts Bay instead on Nov. 21. The passengers established the village of Plymouth at the southern end of the bay around Christmastime.

Moored in the New World for the winter, the Mayflower left the colony on April 5, 1621. It arrived in London without difficulty and its subsequent history is unknown.

In 1957, a replica of the *Mayflower* was built and sailed from England to the United States—in 13 fewer days than its 17th century predecessor. The *Mayflower II* now sits in Plymouth Harbor.

May street is the home of Westside Employment, a social service agency that focuses on adult education and literacy.

Miller Street

(1130 west)

Where can you get a quart of beer for 12-1/2 cents? Or a pint of whiskey for 18-3/4 cents? There is no place in Chicago that can boast of such prices now of course, but at one time at the Forks Tavern, Chicagoans could drink their fill for pennies.

The year was 1831, and the tavern was owned by Samuel Miller, after whom Miller Street is named.

Miller married Elizabeth Kinzie in 1826, and the couple settled at Wolf Point, where the Chicago River branches off near the present site of the Merchandise Mart. The Apparel Center now is located where the Millers once lived.

The couple kept a small store there, and in 1830 they enlarged the structure and turned it into Chicago's second tavern/hotel.

Miller ran a ferry boat across the Chicago River at the present site of Lake Street. At the time, there were no bridges in Chicago, and Miller's ferry boat was the only mode of transportation, other than swimming, available for crossing the waterway. Miller wisely ran the ferry near his tavern, thereby helping both of his businesses.

Miller sold the ferry in 1831, and the next year built Chicago's first bridge near what is now the corner of Kinzie and Canal streets. Designed only for foot traffic, the bridge consisted merely of ropes and logs.

Cook County was organized in March 1831, and Miller was elected to the county's first three-man board of commissioners. The next month, the board awarded Chicago's first two tavern licenses, and Miller received one of them. The liquor license, which cost $5, required that tavern owners charge the prices mentioned earlier for liquor, as well as 37-1/2 cents for each meal served.

Miller was hired by the county to construct Chicago's first public building. Called the "Estray-Pen," the edifice was constructed without a roof, although plans had called for one. Miller thus became the first contractor in Chicago to fail to provide the quality of work his contract had called for. However, unlike the contractors of the future who would dishonestly cut corners, Miller scrupulously refused to accept almost half the money that had been promised to him, because of the inferior work that had been done.

In the spring of 1832, fear of an impending Indian raid drove the Millers and most other Chicagoans to move into Fort Dearborn. Soon after, Elizabeth Miller died, and Samuel Miller sold his tavern and moved to Michigan City, Ind.

Monroe Street

(100 south)

During the 1990s and up to the tragic events of September 11, 2001, Americans had the dubious distinction of living in one of the most politically bitter and partisan eras of the country's existence. An era of no partisanship, in which everybody liked the president and looked forward to the future, seemed almost impossible to imagine during that time.

Yet such a time, which historians call "The Era of Good Feelings," did exist during the 1817-25 Presidency of James Monroe, for whom Monroe Street is named.

Like latter-day counterpart Bill Clinton, Monroe was a former Southern governor who had made his share of mistakes. In Ambassadorial posts under Presidents George Washington and Thomas Jefferson, he had angered his bosses so much that he was relieved of duty each time.

With the War of 1812 going badly, President James Madison called on Virginia Governor James Monroe to join his cabinet. Madison had Monroe reorganize the war department, and the United States ended up beating the British.

With the war won, Americans were feeling good and looking forward to the future. Unbelievably, there wasn't much for Americans to argue about politically, and one of the two major political parties, the Federalist Party, disbanded. That left America as a one-party state for the only time in its existence, and paved the way for Monroe to win two terms in the Presidency with no more than token opposition.

Spain still owned Florida at the beginning of Monroe's first term, and tensions between the two countries caused U.S. General Andrew Jackson to invade Florida twice. Finally, Monroe decided just to buy Florida.

South America was getting tired of Spain as well, and revolts broke out in Spanish colonies all over the hemisphere. This prompted Monroe to issue what became the cornerstone of American foreign policy, the Monroe Doctrine, which said that the Western Hemisphere was to be considered off limits to colonizers from the European powers.

So it's ironic that Monroe Street in Chicago is now being "colonized," as individuals from different areas are moving into new houses and converted lofts while what was once an industrial area becomes residential. With the neighborhood being spruced up, repopulated, and upgraded as a result, one could say that this is an "Era of Good Feelings" on Monroe Street as well.

Morgan Street

(1000 west)

One of many streets in Chicago named for land barons, Morgan derives its name from Thomas Morgan, who once owned 3,000 acres of land on the South Side.

Morgan, however, was not a real estate developer. The Englishman was a farmer, and used the land for agriculture until his death.

He built a homestead called "The Upwood" on the Far South Side near the area that is now called Morgan Park, which also is named for him. An oddity in Chicago, Morgan Park's streets, instead of being laid out on a grid pattern like most of the city's thoroughfares, wind and curve, deliberately designed to do so by Morgan's countryman Thomas F. Nichols.

Newberry Avenue

(828 west)

If Walter L. Newberry, the man for whom Newberry Avenue was named, were to come back from the hereafter, he would likely have two pieces of advice: get a good education, and don't die while away from your home city.

Newberry was a real estate developer, banker, and railroad executive. His love of education was shown in life by his accepting the presidency of the Chicago Board of Education, and at his death in 1868 by his leaving more than $2 million to found the Newberry Library.

Located at 60 W. Walton Street, the Newberry is one of only 15 major independent research libraries in the United States and draws researchers from all over the world. Concentrating on the humanities, the library also has an impressive collection of rare books, maps, and manuscripts.

The Newberry has a particularly good book conservation library and conservation laboratory, which was able to spread out in the older part of the library when a newer building was opened in 1982.

Walter Newberry was travelling by boat to Paris when he died, and his remains were shipped back to Chicago in the handiest container available—a liquor barrel. Despite his wealth, he was inexplicably buried in this makeshift coffin.

Oakley Boulevard

(2300 west)

No, the street is not named for the basketball player. The Charles Oakley that is this thoroughfare's namesake was a trustee of the Illinois and Michigan Canal in the 1840s.

The lot at 815 S. Oakley is the surprising site of a Vietnam veterans' memorial. Near West Sider and Vietnam vet William Lavicka had renovated several buildings on the block, and saved one empty lot for his survivors' memorial, which he created on his own without government help.

Two Buddhist dragons standing on red columns mark the entrance that features a marble path leading to ten larger red cast-iron columns encircling a concrete disc that features a mosaic map of Vietnam.

O'Brien Street

(1244 south)

O'Brien is another street for which city records conflict concerning its naming.

The street may honor James S. O'Brien, an Irish immigrant, landowner, subdivider, and coal commissioner who served as alderman of the 9th Ward from 1871 to 1879.

However, records indicate it also may be named for George O'Brien, who served as a county assessor in 1848.

Ogden Avenue

(diagonal)

Ogden Avenue, which touches the Near West Side near the intersection of Damen Avenue and Polk Street, was named for the city's first mayor, William B. Ogden.

Ogden was one of the primary founders of Chicago. Not only was he the first mayor, but he was a railroad builder, lumber and iron magnate, canal builder, college president, real estate speculator, and bank president.

He was born in the frontier forests of Delaware County, N.Y., in 1805. Growing up in the backwoods, Ogden became an expert rifleman, fisherman, and trapper, and graduated from a log schoolhouse.

At age 16, Ogden became the head of his family due to the death of his father, so he had to go to work and set aside his dream of becoming a lawyer. He found that he had a head for business, and he became so popular in his area that he was elected to the New York State Legislature.

In 1835, Ogden was working for the American Land Company, a real estate firm, and the company sent him to Chicago as its agent. Again, Ogden quickly became popular with his neighbors, and when Chicago was chartered as a city two years later, it was natural that he would be nominated and elected the city's first mayor.

Ogden proved to be a good choice, as during a terrible financial panic he almost single-handedly saved the financial solvency of the city. During the panic, people called for the city not to pay its debts, thinking that the ensuing tax relief would allow the citizens to pull through hard times. A public meeting was called to enact this, but a speech by Ogden persuaded the people to tighten their belts and let the city honor its debts, preserving the municipality as a good credit risk for bankers.

Ogden built the first railroad to come into Chicago, the Galena & Chicago Union (later the Chicago and North Western). His goal was to make Chicago the railroad hub of the Midwest. He later became the first president of the Union Pacific railroad.

He retired in 1875, and married at the age of 70. Ogden spent his retirement back in New York State, dying in his mansion on the Harlem River in 1877.

Ogden Avenue was once one of the major thoroughfares in Chicago. It was one of the first "paved" roads in the area, the pavement being planks. Ogden Avenue, therefore, was originally called Southwestern Plank Road.

As the neighborhoods it runs through began to deteriorate, Ogden Avenue became less important. Although the street once stretched from the southwestern suburbs all the way to Clark Street between Armitage and Fullerton on the North Side, redevelopment in that trendy neighborhood has resulted in the street being blocked off or eliminated altogether a few blocks south of Division Street.

Much news is created on the Near West Side by what the *Gazette* often calls a "decision in a vacuum." A city, state, or federal bureaucrat, often with a politically well-connected developer involved, makes a decision on property reassignment without telling the neighborhood, or sometimes even the owner of the property, first.

An example covered by the *Gazette* was the fight over a proposed Popeye's restaurant at 2822 W. Ogden on land reserved for the Illinois Medical Center to develop and expand medical facilities.

In 1982, the city erroneously issued a building permit to Popeye's, then had to revoke it after a ruling by Cook County Circuit Court Judge James Murray, which pointed out that the Illinois Medical Center had jurisdiction. So in June, 1985, the city did it again—without informing Medical Center officials or the judge, who first learned of it over morning coffee when he opened his *Chicago Tribune.*

Legal battles continued for three more years, until a county court ruled once and for all that the Medical Center, which didn't love that chicken from Popeye's, had the right to determine the course of the land within its boundaries and keep the restaurant out.

Paulina Street

(1700 west)

Paulina is named for Paulina Tayler, a woman who was one of Chicago's earliest farmers and respected citizens.

Born in Quebec, Canada, Paulina Edy married Reuben Tayler, a captain in the Canadian militia, in 1820. In 1838, the couple moved to Chicago, which had been incorporated as a city only a year earlier. Although Chicago was a "city" in name, there was plenty of farmland available within the city limits. The Taylers homesteaded a farm at what is now the area around Ashland Avenue and Madison Street.

The Taylers farmed for many years, and eventually Reuben Tayler entered Chicago's booming real estate business. It was in this field that the family fortune was made, and as leading citizens of Chicago, the Taylers became involved in improving the city in a variety of ways. It was through the Taylers' real estate firm that Union Park was created.

Members of the Episcopal Church, the Taylers had four children, three daughters and a son.

In the Taylers' lifetime, the Chicago City Council honored them by naming streets that originated on their farm Reuben (at 1600 west) and Paulina (at 1700 west). The wealthy denizens of society who lived on Reuben, after suffering "Hey, Rube!" taunts from the less well-to-do, petitioned the City Council to change the name of the street to Ashland. When this was done, the ordinance became the great grief of both of the Taylers.

Paulina Tayler's street retains her name, however. She outlived her husband and, as she had lived a life dedicated to the welfare of the city, died highly esteemed by her fellow Chicagoans—even the "rubes" residing on Ashland.

Peoria Street

(900 west)

"Will it play in Peoria?" was a phrase coined by a member of the staff of Richard Nixon's White House in urging his cohorts to keep in mind the effects of their policies on the heartland of America. Peoria Street, located at 900 west, was once in the heartland of the Near West Side, but time and the University of Illinois at Chicago have wrought their changes.

The construction of UIC obliterated Peoria Street between Harrison Street and Roosevelt Road. If it still existed there, the thoroughfare would run down the center of the campus. Now, Peoria Street touches the Near West Side only as it picks up north of the Eisenhower Expressway and south of the Maxwell Street Market.

Peoria Street is named for the city of Peoria, Ill. "Peoria" is a word coined in the days of trade between the French and the Indians in the 1600s. It means both "leader" and "man carrying a pack."

The city is located about halfway between Chicago and St. Louis. The French built Fort Creve Coeur there in 1680, and extensive French settlement began there around 1711. The area remained the dominion of that ethnic group until 1813, when the U.S. government built Fort Clark there. The fort brought settlers of other ethnic backgrounds to the area, and it was incorporated as a town in 1835. Peoria was chartered as a city in 1845.

Located in Illinois' agricultural and mining belt, Peoria sits on the Illinois River and at the crossroads of several railroads. It is therefore a leading shipping, distributing, and trading center and one of Illinois' larger municipalities. The city also is home to several manufacturing concerns and Bradley University. A research laboratory built by the U.S. Department of Agriculture in 1940 was the site of landmark research concerning penicillin in the 1940s and 1950s.

Across the river from the city proper is Fort Creve Coeur State Monument, containing Fort Creve Coeur. The French explorer who established the fort was Robert Cavalier de La Salle, who also explored what is now Chicago and after whom La Salle Street is named.

Polk Street

(800 south)

"Who is James K. Polk?" is a question that was asked in 1844, and also might be asked today.

Polk Street is named after the 11th president of the United States. James K. Polk was the first so-called "darkhorse" presidential candidate when nominated by the Democratic Party in 1844; almost no one anywhere other than in his home state of Tennessee had ever heard of him.

Despite his lack of notoriety, he won the presidency by beating Henry Clay, one of the 19th century's most prominent politicians. Polk's previous experience included seven terms in the House of Representatives and one term as governor of Tennessee.

Polk was regarded by 19th century historians as a mediocre president, but modern historians rate him as among the top ten chief executives. He entered the presidency with four objectives: reduction of tariffs; creation of an independent treasury for the United States; settlement of the Oregon boundary with English Canada; and the acquisition of California.

He achieved all four, creating economic prosperity that lasted over a decade and adding over 500,000 square miles to the area of the United States. He avoided war with England over Oregon, and presided over the successful conclusion of the war between the United States and Mexico.

Polk declined to run for a second term, and died four months after leaving office in 1849.

The Chicago Cubs played their home games at the West Side Grounds on Polk at Wolcott Street between 1893 and 1915. Despite the Chicago National Leaguers losing their first game there to the Cincinnati Reds 13-12 on May 14, 1893, the *Chicago Tribune* called the park "the best in the world" and estimated the crowd at 13,500. The game was played on a Sunday, and the umpire refused to officiate due to religious reasons, so a replacement had to be found. The Reds' manager was Near West Sider Charles Comiskey.

The Cubs won four pennants at the West Side Grounds, including three straight in 1906-08. The 1906 club still holds the major league record of 116 games won in a single season (since matched by the Seattle

79

Mariners in 2001), and was the only Cub club to play the Chicago White Sox in the World Series.

Cub pitchers threw two no-hitters at the West Side Grounds, and opponents' pitchers hurled three, including one by New York Giant great Christy Mathewson.

It's been a long time since the Cubs played major league baseball on the Near West Side. Of course, some might argue that it's been a long time since the Cubs played major league baseball anywhere.

Between Oakley Boulevard on the west and Damen Avenue on the east, Polk Street is the home of Chicago Technology Park, which provides an array of services and facilities that encourages and develops high technology and biotechnical firms.

Polk Street also is the location of a park that honors "the George Washington of Italy." Garibaldi Park at 1326 W. Polk Street honors Giuseppe Garibaldi, the Italian freedom fighter who unified the Italian nation in 1860.

Racine Street

(1200 west)

Racine Street is named for Jean-Baptiste Racine, a French playwright and poet famous for his tragic plays about ancient Greek heroes and heroines. Racine was born in 1639 and died in Paris in 1699. Orphaned as a small child, he was educated by Jansenist churchmen.

Under the Jansenists, Racine became a great Greek scholar and also studied philosophy. Jansenists, Roman Catholic reformers who accepted such Protestant ideas as predestination, believed that human nature was inherently evil because of the fall of Adam and Eve in the Garden of Eden, and that people could do nothing good without the direct intervention of grace.

Racine's family expected him to become a cleric, but when he became friends with the irreligious and unconventional poet Jean de La Fontaine, they became worried that he would reject the career they had planned for him. Finally, they sent him to live with an uncle who was vicar-general of a cathedral; they hoped that studying theology under his uncle's influence would make Racine give up his worldly ways.

In 1663, however, after two years with his uncle, Racine gave up the church and went to Paris. He was presented at King Louis XIV's court and even wrote a poem in honor of the king's marriage. After that, he had the support and favor of the king and so began to write plays.

His first play was produced the next year, and between 1667 and 1677 he wrote his greatest works, including *Andromaque, Iphigenie,* and *Britannicus.*

Phedre, which is considered his masterpiece, tells the story of a woman who is hopelessly in love with her stepson. True to his Jansenist upbringing, Racine makes the woman helpless in her passion and predestined to destruction. When Phedre learns that her husband (who was believed dead) is living and her stepson is in love with another woman, she is helpless to control her homicidal jealousy and is destroyed by overwhelming guilt.

Even though his plays were successful, Racine gave up the theatre because a strong group of hostile critics praised a writer named Pradon and attacked Racine. In spite of the critics, Pradon is forgotten, while Racine is considered France's greatest classical dramatist.

Not much is known of Racine's personal life during the time he wrote his plays because his relatives burned his letters after his death. It is known, however, that after leaving the theatre around 1678, Racine reconciled with his relatives and married happily. His wife bore seven children; their second son, Louis, became a respected poet and critic.

Racine's plays are outstanding examples of French tragic drama. They are noted for their graceful, poetic use of the French language, which contrasts sharply with the violence and evil of the characters. The plays also are important because Racine's characters, who were taken from Greek tragedy and from history, are very realistic and think and act like people in the modern world.

There's just something about that Harrison-Racine area that creates Near West Side news. The northwest corner also was home for many years to one of the worst-designed malls ever. Built by National Republic Bank at 500 S. Racine in 1974, and called Circle Court Mall or Chicago Galleria over the years, the mall's lack of windows on the outside made it look like a factory, and its massive concrete ramps on the inside kept what few customers there were from being able to find, or even see, the stores.

For a while the mall held its own financially thanks to the City of Chicago renting space in it for several municipal offices, but when the city pulled out in 1982 it sent the mall careening from one unworkable plan to another. At the end of that year it was acquired by Dallas-based conglomerate Southmark Corp., whose real-estate expertise was wasted on a facility plagued by questionable design, security problems, and some bizarre tenants.

In 1987 the mall was put up for sale, then quickly withdrawn from the market, showing that even mighty Southmark was scratching its collective head over what to do with the architectural oddity. Finally, Southmark did sell the mall to LaMancha/Circle Court Associates of North Carolina.

This outfit fared no better with the white elephant and in 1991 sold it to the University of Illinois at Chicago, which has finally put the facility to good use as a student services building.

Roosevelt Road

(1200 south)

"The Trust Buster." "The Rough Rider." "The Hero of San Juan Hill."

These are some of the nicknames that were given to Theodore Roosevelt, 26th president of the United States and the man for whom Roosevelt Road was named.

The most athletic of all presidents, Roosevelt was born weak and asthmatic in New York City in 1858. Sickly, puny "Teedie," after being roughed up at the age of ten by some tougher boys, began exercising in a gym, and continued to work out for the rest of his life. He learned boxing, judo, horseback riding, tennis, and shooting, among other sports.

At the age of 25, Roosevelt, finding New York City too stifling, moved to South Dakota and bought two cattle ranches. During a barroom brawl in the Dakotas in which a cowboy came at him with two pistols, Roosevelt beat the cowboy into unconsciousness with his bare hands.

Although he had been a Republican politician and government official, Roosevelt first gained widespread notoriety as a lieutenant colonel in the Spanish-American War of 1898. He organized a cavalry unit, the "Rough Riders," and led the famous charge up San Juan Hill, which made him a national hero.

He parlayed this fame into a successful run for governor of New York State, and upon taking office immediately promoted a civil service law and a corporate tax. These reforms scared conservative Republican bigwigs, so they decided to get rid of the progressive Roosevelt by pushing him for vice president of the United States in the election of 1900.

When Roosevelt got the nomination, political boss Mark Hanna told President William McKinley, "Now, it is up to you to live." He didn't, dying in September 1901, and Roosevelt became president.

He got off to a running start. Roosevelt settled a war between Russia and Japan, supported a revolution in Panama to secure construction of the Panama Canal, and initiated action to dismantle the J.P. Morgan Northern Securities trust, becoming the first president to try to break up big business. He was reelected for a second term in 1904 by a huge popular vote.

After another frenetic four years, Roosevelt, in following precedent set by all other presidents who had served up to that time, declined to run for a third term. His close political associate, William Howard Taft, was elected president in 1908.

The progressive Roosevelt felt that Taft was too conservative as president, and endeavored to wrest the 1912 Republican nomination from him. Roosevelt failed, so he formed a third party, the "Bull Moose Party," and ran for president anyway. During a campaign speech in Milwaukee he was shot by a lunatic, but finished his speech before allowing himself to be taken to the hospital.

Roosevelt was beaten for the presidency by Woodrow Wilson, but he had come in second, the first and only minor party candidate ever to do so in a presidential race. Taft finished a distant third.

Roosevelt lived a robust sporting life until he died suddenly at age 60 in 1919. Shortly thereafter, the Chicago City Council decided to rename 12th Street in his honor.

The street was famous in the 19th century for its involvement with another president. In 1865 it was the first road Abraham Lincoln's funeral cortege moved down in Chicago after the late president's corpse was removed from the train that brought it to the city. Chicago in 1861 had given Lincoln enough votes to earn a majority in Illinois, and as a result, the presidency.

A major business thoroughfare for most of its existence, Roosevelt Road on the Near West Side fell upon hard times in the latter part of the 20th century, becoming lined with boarded-up stores and empty lots. An exception to the general dilapidation was the R&R Clinic Medical Center at 1231 W. Roosevelt, built in 1996 to serve the area's low-income population—the first new commercial construction in the area in more than half a century.

When the clinic's builders were requesting a construction permit, the city granted it, but forgot one little thing. The owners were not told that the area was being considered for rezoning as residential. Only two years later, the "city that works" decided it wanted the property through eminent domain to build residential housing on what always had been a business strip.

Sangamon Street

(932 west)

The name of Sangamon Street honors the Midwest's American Indian heritage.

"Sangamon" was the way the area's early settlers of European heritage mispronounced the Algonquian Indian word "sagamo," which means "chief" in many Algonquian languages.

The Algonquian Indian family originally was made up of several hundred tribes who spoke 50 similar languages. Among the tribes making up the Algonquian family are ones familiar from history such as the Algonquin, the Blackfoot, the Mohican, and the Potawatami. They lived in the area of the United States extending from the East Coast to the Rocky Mountains and from Canada to the modern states of North Carolina and Tennessee.

Algonquian tribes attached great importance to familial and clan relationships as well as to religious philosophy and ceremonies. They cultivated wild rice and therefore were the area's first farmers.

Rivals to the Algonquian in this geographical area were the Iroquois, who were the most highly organized Indians, and who had a unique governmental structure that included a council of women who elected chiefs, had the power to declare war, and approved all important actions.

Most "sagamo," as in the case of the aforementioned Iroquois, did not come to their positions as chiefs through inheritance, as European monarchs did, but were elected through vote or trial. In any case, tribal chiefs did not possess absolute authority, so their powers were more like those of modern-day chief executives rather than like those of the European kings and queens who were their contemporaries.

The Algonquian Potawatami were the most powerful Indians in the area that is now Chicago when the missionary Father Jacques Marquette and the explorer Louis Jolliet became the first individuals of European heritage to explore the area and help secure France's claim to it in 1673.

Ninety years later, the area was ceded to the British, and 20 years after that the area technically became part of the United States, although the Indians still claimed the land as theirs and prevented most non-Indians from settling there.

After the U.S. forces of General "Mad Anthony" Wayne defeated Indian forces at the Battle of Fallen Timbers in Ohio, the ensuing Treaty of Greenville included a provision whereby the Indians officially ceded the land that runs from what is now Fullerton Avenue to 31st Street, and Cicero Avenue to Lake Michigan, to the United States. The army built Fort Dearborn at what is now Michigan Avenue and Wacker Drive in 1803.

The Indians continued to fight sporadically with settlers, driving them completely out of the area between 1812 and 1816, until the conclusion of the Black Hawk War in 1832. The treaty concluding that war called for the Indians to be paid to relocate west of the Mississippi River. Final payments were made in Chicago in 1835, at which time 800 Indians participated in one last dance of defiance within the town limits before giving up their claim to the area forever.

Sangamon Street is home to Haymarket House, which ministers to the needs of alcoholics, addicts, the homeless, and others of society's less fortunate. It is the fruition of the life's work of a Chicago icon, Monsignor Ignatius "Father Mac" McDermott.

Taylor Street

(1000 south)

Taylor Street has a unique, eccentric character all its own. So it is appropriate that the main business strip of the Near West Side should be named after a unique, eccentric president of the United States who would have dramatically changed American history had he lived to complete his term.

Zachary Taylor became a general in the United States Army despite the fact that he rarely wore an army uniform, and he was elected president despite never having voted in his life.

Taylor preferred to wear farm clothing or a business suit when he led his troops into battle. During the Mexican War in 1847, "Old Rough and Ready" and his army of 5,000 defeated the Mexican army of 20,000 at the battle of Buena Vista, making Taylor a national hero.

He was nominated for the presidency in 1848 by the now-defunct Whig Party. Taylor was not particularly interested in running for office, and refused to accept the letter informing him of his nomination because it came to his home postage due. He won the election nonetheless, and became the 12th president of the United States.

The most important political issue of the time was the problem of how to deal with slavery in the territories that had been acquired from Mexico during the war. Taylor, although a Southerner, opposed the extension of slavery into the new territories.

A series of eight laws favoring the Southern proslavery viewpoint were introduced in the Senate in 1850. Taylor intended to veto the bills, and was told by three Southern congressmen that the South would break away from the Union if he did so. Taylor informed the Congressmen that he would not permit Southern secession, and that he intended to personally lead the Union troops in battle against the South.

Had Taylor lived to veto the bills, it is almost a certainty that the Civil War would have begun a decade earlier than it did. It also is a virtual certainty that Taylor would have ended the Civil War quickly, because he was a much better military tactician than any of the generals President Abraham Lincoln was forced to use when the Civil War occurred. Taylor would have gone down in history as one of America's greatest heroes, instead of someone of whom the average person has no knowledge.

Taylor, however, became ill from eating too much ice cream and cherries on a hot day, and died from acute gastroenteritis on July 9, 1850. His successor, President Millard Fillmore, signed the eight bills, which became known as the Compromise of 1850, thereby postponing the Civil War for ten years.

The president for whom the Near West Side's main street was named was back in the news in 1991 when writer Clara Rising penned a biography of Taylor. In it, she engaged in unprecedented speculation that Senator and former Secretary of State Henry Clay or Vice President Fillmore had murdered Taylor. Calling a secretary of state and vice president murderers often is a good way to get publicity for a new book, but there is another surefire method: dig up a dead president's corpse.

This is exactly what Rising paid more than $1,200 for, getting Taylor's body exhumed from its crypt to be poked and prodded by medical examiners looking for "evidence" that the president had been murdered. As this event happened during the summer of 1991, what members of the media call "the silly season" when little news is being made and publications editors and news show directors look for odd stories to fill up their productions, publicity abounded.

Medical examiners, as one might have predicted, concluded emphatically that President Taylor had not been murdered. Zachary Taylor once again rests in peace, with his bones no longer the object of America's curiosity, as if they were no different than Michael Jackson's sequined glove or Madonna's bra.

One of the earliest scandals reported by the *Gazette* concerned Taylor Street. In 1982, two private homes on the 1300 block of west Taylor were cited for acquisition by the Chicago Department of Housing, to be given to a developer. The City Council approved the plan the next year.

So what was the scandal? Not only did all involved never bother to acquire the properties, the *Gazette* reported in 1984, but they never even informed the owners of the proceedings, either.

With Mayor Harold Washington's appointment of Brenda J. Gaines as housing commissioner, the decision was reversed and the families kept their homes.

One of the homes belonged to Albert and Theresa Prisco, who had gained statewide attention in 1974 when they became the first merchants in state history licensed to sell Illinois lottery tickets, in their coffee shop located—where else?—on Taylor Street.

President Bill Clinton, with his weakness for a good meal, early in his presidency on a trip to Chicago went to Tuscany Restaurant on Taylor Street with Mayor Richard M. Daley to sample the northern Italian cuisine. He even posed for a photo shoot with a baby belonging to a family having dinner there at the time.

Clinton, like Jimmy Carter before him, is no stranger to the Near West Side, having been the only presidential candidate to campaign there in 1992.

Throop Street

(1300 west)

Do you enjoy a glass of wine with dinner? An after-dinner cordial? A beer during the ballgame?

If so, the man for whom Throop Street is named would not be happy with your choice of beverage.

Amos G. Throop was a leading lumberman in Chicago over a century ago. As did many of Chicago's founders who made their fortunes in other endeavors, Throop got involved in both politics and social causes. In politics, he served as a common counselor (alderman). In the area of social betterment, he served in the temperance movement.

Crusades against "demon rum" were common in the 19th century. "Temperance" is actually a misnomer, since most of its advocates appealed for total abstinence from the drinking of liquor.

Agitation for temperance in the United States began in earnest in the 1820s with the establishment of hundreds of temperance societies. Temperance orators attempted to use personal appeals to get people to stop drinking and "sign the pledge," in which they promised never to drink again. In the 1840s, the Washington Society, a group of reformed alcoholics, organized lodges throughout the country to keep alcoholics from drinking again—setting the example for today's Alcoholics Anonymous organization.

As the temperance movement gained strength, demands that liquor sales be made illegal began to be voiced. By 1851, the temperance forces had succeeded in prohibiting liquor in Maine, and had also won victories in certain parts of other states.

Throop headed one of six temperance organizations in Chicago in 1855. He and his fellow leaders called liquor a "blighting curse" and wrote that if Illinois were to pass a prohibition law, "Thousands will weep…tears of joy, of gladness, and of hope."

The Civil War pushed the temperance issue out of the spotlight; investment in the liquor trade increased almost sevenfold between 1860 and 1880, as people drank to forget their wartime and postwar troubles. Cities like Chicago, with big populations of immigrants from countries in which liquor was an important and respected part of the culture (such as

Ireland, Germany, and Italy), contained one saloon for every 200 inhabitants.

It wasn't until the latter part of the century that the prohibition movement began to achieve and surpass the power of the pre-war temperance agitation, succeeding in making liquor illegal in five states by 1900. By the beginning of World War I, two-thirds of the states were dry and by 1919, Congress passed and a majority of states ratified the 18th Amendment, making liquor illegal all over the United States.

What the early temperance crusaders failed to foresee was the rise in crime and gangsterism that prohibition would bring. Bootleggers like Al Capone thrived on the illegal liquor trade, and branched out into other illegal activities as well.

By the 1930s, the average citizen wanted an end to prohibition and to bootleggers' illegal activities. Shortly after Franklin Roosevelt became president in 1933, Congress and the states concurred in repealing the 18th amendment, spiriting away Amos Throop's dream once and for all.

Tilden Street

(420 south)

Tilden, located at 420 south, no longer is much of a street. The Eisenhower Expressway eliminated most of it from the map. Small strips of Tilden are left just north of some parts of the Eisenhower.

Just as Tilden Street has been forgotten by most Near West Siders, so Samuel J. Tilden had mostly been forgotten by history—until the 2000 presidential election brought his name back into the news for the first time in more than a century.

Tilden should have been the 19th president of the United States. Indeed, he won the presidential election of 1876 by about 250,000 votes, yet he was not permitted to take office.

In 1876, after two terms of Republican Ulysses S. Grant's corrupt presidential administration, Americans were ready for a Democratic president. The Democratic Party nominated popular reformer Samuel J. Tilden, governor of New York, for the presidency. The Republicans nominated the equally respectable but uninspiring Rutherford B. Hayes of Ohio to face Tilden.

During this, the post-Reconstruction period, politics in some Southern states resembled what Chicago's Council Wars would be during the administration of Mayor Harold Washington. Two factions that hated each other struggled for power, and each held some control.

The president of the United States is not elected by popular vote, as the country learned in 2000. Instead, Americans actually vote for "electors" who are constitutionally responsible for choosing the president.

When the two warring factions in Florida, Louisiana, and South Carolina saw that the popular vote was close, each sent in different sets of election returns to the Federal government, one set showing that Tilden had won, and the other set asserting that Hayes was the victor.

If Tilden, who had 184 undisputed electoral votes, had gotten one more, he'd have had a majority and would have been named president. Lacking that vote, and with the returns of the three states in dispute, the result was that no president was elected.

To deal with the matter, Congress created an electoral commission of eight Republicans and seven Democrats. They voted strictly along party lines, and named Hayes president, despite more people having voted for Tilden.

In return for not continuing the electoral fight in the courts, the Democrats were promised that federal occupation troops in Florida, Louisiana, and South Carolina, which had been stationed there since the end of the Civil War 11 years before, would be removed, giving control of the local governments of those states to the Democrats.

While the compromise avoided possible bloodshed, it resulted in Blacks losing all political power in the South, as the Democrats in the region at that time were committed to White supremacy. The legacy of this compromise was decades of repression and violence directed against Blacks.

The presidential election of 1876 was the sorriest example of cheating in American history, until 2000 lay claim to the distinction. Tilden, presumably disgusted by the whole thing, refused in two subsequent elections to run, even though the nomination would have been his for the asking.

Tilden left a great part of his fortune to fund and endow the New York Public Library system. He died in 1886.

Union Street

(700 west)

Union Street was named not for the American labor movement, but for the union of the United States of America.

Although the nation no longer often is called "the Union," the question of the United States remaining a union was the nation's most significant problem through the Civil War.

When the 13 colonies defeated the British in the Revolutionary War in 1783, they were allied under the "Articles of Confederation," but the "union" was a weak one. Inhabitants of these newly independent states thought of them more as independent countries than as part of one larger nation. One of the reasons the founders created the U.S. Constitution in 1789, therefore, was "in order to form a more perfect Union."

Although the Constitution strengthened the Union, different sections of the country began to develop their own interests and from time to time threatened to secede from, or dissolve, the Union.

With four of the first five presidents of the United States hailing from the South, the New England states between 1789 and 1824 often threatened to secede from the Union. New Englanders felt that the Southerners were promoting policies that favored the agricultural South at the expense of the manufacturing and commercial New England states.

New England's fervor for secession died in 1824 with the passage of a tariff bill that, though badly written, protected the rights of Northern manufacturers. But by this time, some Southerners were agitating for disunion over the questions of extension of slavery and states' rights. States' righters believed that individual states could nullify federal laws, a position with which federal officials obviously disagreed.

The major pre-Civil War threat to the Union came in 1850, when Southerners and Northerners clashed over extension of slavery into territories acquired during the Mexican War. President Zachary Taylor, although a Southerner, was adamant about not letting the South have its way. But when he died suddenly, his successor, President Millard Fillmore, signed a compromise bill Congress had worked out, and the Union was preserved for another decade.

That period allowed the quarrel over slavery to simmer in bitterness, and in 1860-61 eleven Southern states decided to dissolve the Union.

President Abraham Lincoln sent troops against them, and the Civil War had begun with the purpose of restoring the Union.

In 1864, when Lincoln, the first Republican president, ran for reelection, he did so not under the banner of the G.O.P. but as the candidate of the party he called the Union Party, as union was the only issue he felt was important. He chose as his vice presidential running mate a Democrat, Andrew Johnson, who also was willing to run under the Union Party rubric.

The history books are sometimes confused as to whether Johnson, who succeeded to the presidency upon Lincoln's assassination, was a Republican or Democratic president. In truth, he was neither; he was a Union president.

It took nearly 500,000 deaths in the Civil War to restore the Union, and the question of dissolving it hadn't risen again until some members of the Southern Party, formed in Southern states in the late 20th century, began to advocate this position once again.

Union Street's name honors the heavily pro-Union sentiment in Chicago before the Civil War.

Van Buren Street

(400 south)

The 1988 election of Vice President George Bush the elder to the presidency brought the name of Martin Van Buren, after whom Van Buren Street is named, into the media spotlight for the first time in nearly 150 years. Van Buren, in 1836, had been the last incumbent vice president before Bush to be elected president of the United States.

Bush's and Van Buren's lives and political careers bore a great degree of similarity. Both were considered East Coast bluebloods, with Democrat Van Buren from upstate New York and Republican Bush originally from Connecticut. Both were criticized for their upper-crust upbringings during their presidential campaigns.

Both were known for their party loyalty rather than strong ideology and for having served their party and government in a variety of posts—in Van Buren's case as presidential nominating convention delegate, United States senator, ambassador to England, and vice president.

Bush, in the 1988 campaign, was criticized for failing to take clear stands on issues, but he looks like an ideologue compared to Van Buren. In the 1830s, the word "vanburenish" was coined to represent non-commitalism. Once, when a senator asked Van Buren if he believed that the sun rises in the East, "Matty" replied, "I understand that's the common acceptance, but as I never get up 'til after dawn, I can't really say."

Both served as vice presidents under extremely popular presidents: Bush with Ronald Reagan and Van Buren with Andrew Jackson. Both ran with vice presidential candidates of their own who were extremely unpopular: Dan Quayle and Richard Johnson.

The parallels between Quayle and Johnson are even stronger than those between Bush and Van Buren. Both the military records and the lady-loves of Quayle and Johnson were controversial. Each man had been offered the number-two spot on his party's ticket because his ideology closely mirrored that of the popular outgoing president. And although Quayle and Johnson each had served in Congress, many people felt neither candidate was qualified to be vice president, and that their parties should have dumped them when their presidential running mates sought second terms.

Quayle is a "hawk" on military matters, but he likely is unaware that Democrat Johnson helped create the term. Johnson, along with Henry Clay and a few others, were the country's original "war hawks," a term coined to describe several Congressmen who promoted war against the British and their American Indian allies in 1812.

Johnson, a true war hero decorated by Congress for his valor, served and was wounded five times in the War of 1812, as a U.S. Army colonel under General William Henry Harrison. Yet when he ran for vice president in 1836, his military record created as much furor as Quayle's in 1988.

It seems that in the Battle of the Thames, the Shawnee Chief Tecumseh was slain. Although at the time the deed was attributed to a private, David King, several months later the story began to circulate that Johnson actually had killed Tecumseh.

Johnson had killed a chief, but proof that that chief was Tecumseh was never conclusive. The colonel and Harrison truly believed that Johnson had personally dispatched the great warrior. Yet when he ran for vice president, Johnson was vilified by his opponents for fabricating the story for political gain, just as Quayle was vilified for staying out of the Vietnam War despite his hawkish views.

Nonetheless, Johnson's supporters were as fervent in their belief in the story as right-wingers in the late 1980s and 1990s were in contributing to Quayle's fundraisers.

In 1990, Vice President Quayle was among many Federal officials given a hefty pay raise, but he found himself at the center of the storm of public anger because many considered him to be a particularly ineffectual individual in a meaningless job. Johnson had found himself at the center of his own pay-related political catastrophe in 1816.

Johnson got the Congress to pass a bill that raised its members' salaries a whopping 60 percent. The resulting furor over the "salary grab act" cost dozens of congressmen their seats in that fall's elections.

Quayle's wife Marilyn, with her apparent intellectual dominance of her husband and her far-right religious beliefs, proved controversial enough during her husband's time on the national stage, but not nearly so much as Johnson's significant other, Julia Chinn. Julia was a slave that the Kentuckian Johnson owned, and the couple lived together as husband and wife "without benefit of clergy," as polite contemporaries said, and raised a family.

Johnson's blissful domestic arrangement made him, as Van Buren's 1836 vice-presidential candidate, the foil for jokesters across the nation. No vice president would be the butt of so many snide attempts at humor until Quayle came on the scene 152 years later.

When Bush needed to offset his East Coast urbanity by choosing a Reaganite running-mate, he picked Quayle. In doing so, he merely followed Van Buren's example, as Matty had decided he needed Jacksonian Richard Johnson to offset his own Eastern upper-crustiness.

The choice of Johnson caused the same mixture of befuddlement and dismay as the choice of Quayle would a century and a half later. Many thought that the choice of the amiable but mediocre sponsor of the salary grab, the favorite target of comedians nationwide, was the worst possible blunder. In an 1836 Democratic convention much more raucous than its 1988 Republican counterpart, Virginia's delegates greeted the nomination of Johnson with hisses and catcalls and walked out.

If, as vice president, Quayle showed more interest in golf than government, he again merely followed in the footsteps of Johnson, who preferred innkeeping to political intrigue. Johnson even took one summer off from his duties in the Capitol to go back to Kentucky to run his tavern.

Van Buren worked much harder than either Quayle or Johnson, but his main contribution to American history was not a great legislative or military accomplishment. Instead, it was the introduction into popular culture of the expression "OK."

Since Van Buren was born in Kinderhook, N.Y., one of his nicknames was "Old Kinderhook," or "OK." On March 27, 1840, the OK Club of New York City, the local Democratic organization, broke in on an opposition Whig Party meeting shouting, "Down with the Whigs boys, OK!" The newspapers picked up use of the expression, and it swept the country, much as "where's the beef?" did a few years ago.

While the expression OK stayed around, Van Buren didn't, as Americans probably wondered "where's the beef?" during his presidency. Voters fed up with economic problems and a silly vice president turned Van Buren out of office when he ran for a second term. In 1992, George Bush the elder would experience Van Buren deja vu.

Bush as an ex-president has wisely kept a lower profile than Matty. Van Buren unsuccessfully sought the Democratic nomination in 1844 and ran a third-party campaign in 1848, but never regained the White House.

Two other incumbent vice presidents who were elected president were John Adams and Thomas Jefferson. Adams, like Van Buren and

Bush, was rejected by the voters the second time around. Jefferson therefore stands alone in American history as a vice president who became a successful, elected two-term chief executive.

Vernon Park Place

(700 south)

The street takes its name from the former moniker of the Near West Side's Arrigo Park. The park had been named for William Vernon, an official of the Illinois Central Railroad who died in 1884. Hardly anyone in the neighborhood calls the park by either name, preferring to use "Peanut Park."

Washburne Street

(1230 south)

Washburne Street is named for a confidant of President Lincoln who was responsible for Ulysses S. Grant becoming a general.

Born in Maine in 1816, Elihu B. Washburne worked as a printer, school teacher, and newspaper reporter before becoming a lawyer. After passing his bar examination in 1840, he moved to Galena, Ill.

With a presidential election that year, Washburne went to work in the ultimately successful campaign of William Henry Harrison. He moved up in the ranks of the Whig Party, and was elected to the U.S. Congress in 1852 where after a few years, like most Whigs, he decided to switch to the Republican Party because of its strong antislavery platform.

In 1855, he became chairperson of the House of Representatives' Committee on Commerce, and soon became known as "the watchdog of the treasury" as he fought against corruption and graft. Well-liked, Washburne was chosen by the House to be the representative to welcome the newly elected President Lincoln to Washington, D.C., in 1861.

Washburne already was one of Lincoln's most trusted friends, and the president relied on him to guide his legislation through Congress.

It was Washburne who first suggested that his fellow Illinoisan, Colonel Ulysses S. Grant, be named a brigadier general. The congressman later helped write and guide passage of the bill making Grant general of all the armies of the U.S.

Washburne, commonly known as the "father of the House" by the end of his career there, also wrote the legislation that created the United States' national cemeteries, including Arlington.

After Grant became president, he appointed Washburne secretary of state and later minister to France. Normally a diplomatic plum, this latter post was a difficult one during Washburne's tenure, as the Franco-Prussian War was being fought while he was in Paris. Washburne's embassy became a refuge for people of all nationalities fleeing the war.

Washburne retired from government in 1876, although he was mentioned as a presidential candidate at the Republican conventions in 1880 and 1884. He moved to Chicago and served as president of the Chicago Historical Society from 1884 to 1887. Hempstead Washburne, his son, was mayor of Chicago from 1891 to 1893.

Washington Boulevard

(100 north)

George Washington, the first president of the United States and the man for whom the street at 100 north is named, in the early days of the republic was regarded as something of a saint or even a second savior sent to do divine work here on Earth. Now, he is portrayed doing everything from waterskiing to munching tacos for President's Day sales.

While he was neither savior or salesman, he was, as one biographer has called him, "The Indispensible Man." For Washington set precedents that created the government we have today—often by what he *didn't* do.

Despite pleas by some that General Washington seize civilian power militarily at the end of the Revolutionary War, his refusal to do set the primacy of civilian over military authority in the United States forever. His refusal to establish a monarchy created the American republic. And, Washington's additional refusal to seek a third term as president has resulted in all but one of his successors doing the same.

Although Washington has been portrayed as a rather cold and somber individual, he once was able to stop a potential coup d'etat against the government through force of emotion. With Army officers ready to overthrow the government after the Revolutionary War because they hadn't been paid, Washington, speaking to the assembled insurgents, tried to read a letter from Congress concerning Army pay, but was unable to. He apologized, saying "I have already grown gray in the service of my country. I am now going blind." His simple declaration of patriotic sacrifice stunned the soldiers and drove them to tears, and the coup d'etat was forgotten.

As president, after appearing before the U.S. Senate a few times during his first year in office for Constitutionally mandated "advice and consent" on treaties and appointments, Washington decided it was a waste of time to show up in person and quit doing so. Except for State of the Union messages, all of Washington's successors have followed this precedent.

As general and president, the properly mannered and classically educated Washington always was the right man in the right place at the right time, doing the right thing. Even in his final illness, he apologized to his doctors and his wife for all the trouble his sickness had caused them (over only two days), and then died.

Western Avenue

(2400 west)

Western Avenue has its name for a very simple reason: it was, when it was named in 1850, the western boundary of the City of Chicago.

Chicago's boundaries have changed greatly over the years. When it was incorporated as a town in 1833, Chicago had a population of approximately 350 living in about 150 wooden houses, and was only 3/8 of a mile square. Borders were Kinzie Street (400 north) on the north, Madison Street (0 north and south) on the south, State Street on the east, and Desplaines Street (700 west) on the west. At the time, black bear still were being killed for food just outside the Loop.

When Chicago was incorporated as a city in 1837, it had a population of approximately 20,000 living in about 3,000 houses, and the city was ten miles square. Boundaries were North Avenue (1600 north) on the north, 22nd Street on the south, Lake Michigan on the east, and Wood Street (1800 west) on the west. By 1850, the population had risen to approximately 30,000.

An author of the period wrote, "The city is situated on both sides of the Chicago River, a sluggish slimy stream, too lazy to clean itself, [with banks] resembling a salt marsh...There was no pavement...no drainage...[and] the people lived [in] small timber buildings painted white, and this white much defeated by mud..."

But Chicago in 1850 already was becoming an industrial and transportation power. The McCormick Reaper factory employed hundreds to build farm machinery. There were abundant clay deposits in Chicago, so bricklaying was an important trade. The Illinois and Michigan Canal had opened two years earlier, and the railroads were just beginning to be built.

In that year therefore, Chicago was well on its way to becoming the "Hog Butcher for the World, Tool Maker, Stacker of Wheat, Player with Railroads, and the Nation's Freight Handler" it would be in the second half of the 19th century.

Such industrial power created the need for more space, and in 1889 the city almost quadrupled its size from 43 miles square to 168 miles square by annexing the towns of Jefferson, Lake View, Lake, and Hyde Park.

Through 1950, the city from time to time annexed small areas bordering it, until its present boundaries took shape. In the 1950s the O'Hare Airport land, located farther away from Western Avenue than anyone in 1850 could have imagined Chicago growing, was annexed, completing the city's present configuration.

Winchester Street

(1950 west)

Winchester is named for a battle of the Civil War that was a prelude to the most famous of them all: the Battle of Gettysburg.

In May of 1863, the Confederate Army scored a stunning victory against the Union Army in the Battle of Chancellorsville, Va. The Northern troops, led by General Joseph Hooker, had been forced to retreat, and this inspired Confederate General Robert E. Lee to attempt invasion of Pennsylvania, which remained in the Union.

A successful invasion, Lee had good reason to believe, might put Northern Democrats who opposed Republican President Abraham Lincoln in a position to end the war on terms that would allow Southern independence. It also would give the under-supplied Southern troops access to Northern food and clothing.

So in June, 1863, Lee moved his troops northward to Gettysburg, Pennsylvania, with Hooker's troops in pursuit. Along the way, the two armies would meet in two smaller battles, one of which was at Winchester, a town of 3,500 residents at the northern end of the Valley and about 65 miles northeast of Washington, D.C.

On the morning of June 13, the Confederate troops of Major General Jubal Early attacked the Union troops of Major General Robert Milroy. Milroy's troops were stationed at Winchester despite the recommendations of Union General-in-Chief Henry Halleck, who wanted them stationed in the safer position of Harper's Ferry, 30 miles away. Milroy, however, insisted his troops could hold Winchester "against any force the Rebels could afford to bring against it."

After the battle began, Milroy withdrew his troops to three forts at the town. The fighting then stopped as the Confederate troops of Brigadier General John Gordon, Lieutenant General Richard Ewell, and Major General Richard Johnson spent the day surrounding the structures.

Shortly after 5 p.m., the Confederates attacked again. Fighting raged through the night, and the Northern troops mounted a charge at about 3:30 a.m., only to be stopped by a Confederate brigade commanded by Brigadier General Maryland Steuart.

At dawn, another Confederate brigade, led by General James A. Walker, joined the fight and the Federals were defeated. A total of 443

Northerners died, and 3,358 were captured. The Confederates also seized some badly needed cannons and wagons.

The Southerners then proceeded to Gettysburg, where they fought the Federals from July 1-3. The North won this battle, and thereby turned around the course of the war. Never again would the Southern troops be strong enough to attack the North, and instead had to retreat to the South where the unavailability of food and armaments doomed them to defeat.

The Chicago City Council named the street not for the Confederate victory, but for the Northern troops who died there.

The Winchester area is famous for its apple production. The land was first mapped out by a young surveyor named George Washington in 1748, and he returned to the town as a general to establish his military headquarters during the French and Indian War of 1754-63.

Wolcott Street

(1900 west)

Since the Near West Side is the site of Chicago's top health care facilities, it is appropriate that Wolcott (1900 west), named for an early Chicago physician, is located in the area.

Dr. Alexander Wolcott was born in Connecticut in 1790 and graduated from Yale University at the age of 19. When he was 30, he joined an expedition that was exploring the rivers that flowed into the Mississippi, and thereby came to Chicago.

The town still was suffering from the effects of the Fort Dearborn Massacre of a few years before, and was sparsely populated. One visitor wrote, "The village presents no cheering prospects...it consists of but few huts, inhabited by a miserable race of men...Their log or bark houses are low, filthy, and disgusting, displaying not the least trace of comfort."

Not all of the residents of the squalid village were men, however. John Kinzie, one of the area's leading citizens, had a 16-year-old daughter, Nell, who caught Wolcott's attention. Alexander and Nell fell in love and Wolcott decided to stay, taking a job as an Indian agent. His assumption of this post also gave Chicago the benefit of having a doctor, which the village had lacked.

The couple married three years later, and the wedding was one of Chicago's first major social events. Anyone who wanted to attend the wedding was welcome to do so, and Indians, French-Canadian traders, travelers, explorers, and army officers all celebrated the marriage.

Later in 1823, the army decided to abandon Fort Dearborn, as it was felt the Indian threat had been neutralized. Dr. and Mrs. Wolcott then decided to move into the abandoned fort, and they lived in high style in the officers' headquarters. In 1828, the army decided to reclaim the fort, so the Wolcotts had to move out.

Dr. Wolcott, a justice of the peace in his later years, died in 1830. Nell Kinzie Wolcott remarried six years later and moved to Detroit, where she died in 1860.

Wood Street

(1800 west)

Wood is yet another street named for a developer, as Alonzo Wood made his fortune in real estate in Chicago in the 1880s.

On Wood at Taylor is the University of Illinois Hospital, the centerpiece of the university's medical center. In January, 1989, the *Near West/South Gazette* reported some stunning news: the university planned to affiliate with Michael Reese Hospital on the Southeast Side for patient care and educational activities and vacate its medical center, turning it over to Cook County Hospital.

This potential abandonment of the Near West Side caused as much of an uproar as when the eastern portion of the campus took over parts of the Near West Side in the 1960s. The strong criticism coupled with a rejection of the plan by the state legislature killed the deal. On its own since then, UIC's medical center has thrived, and is now considered a world-class health care institution.

Praise for Streets of the Near West Side:

"I applaud you for making your experiences with the world's greatest city available for the rest of us to enjoy."

—Richard J. Durbin, United States Senator from Illinois

"It's great! I loved it!"

—Rev. Robert P. Rousseau, SSS, Center for Eucharistic Evangelizing, Houston, TX, and former pastor, Notre Dame de Chicago Church, Near West Side, Chicago

"I really enjoyed it. It's got a lot of information that even people who've been in the neighborhood a long time aren't aware of."

—Mary Anne Piemonte, Near West Side Resident

A "fine contribution to Chicago journalism."

—Alderman Burton Natarus, Chicago City Council

About the Authors

William S. Bike, a professional journalist since 1979, has served as associate editor of the *Near West/South Gazette*, an independent community newspaper in Chicago, since 1983. He also is associate director of advancement for the College of Dentistry at the University of Illinois at Chicago. Previously, he has been employed as publications director for the University of Chicago Graduate School of Business and for Loyola University Chicago, where he and his staff won 39 local, national, and international publication awards. In addition, for his writing for the *Near West/South Gazette*, Bike has won three Peter Lisagor Awards from the Chicago Headline Club, the local chapter of the Society of Professional Journalists. The Lisagor is the highest award in Chicago journalism. His freelance articles have appeared in the *Chicago Sun-Times*, *Nine: A Journal of Baseball History and Social Policy Perspectives*, and many more publications. Bike is the author of the first edition of *Streets of the Near West Side*, ACTA Publications, Chicago, 1996, and Winning Political Campaigns, Denali Press, Juneau, Alaska, 1998 and 2001. He also is the editor of *Essays on Earl Renfroe—A Man of Firsts*, UIC College of Dentistry Press, 2001. A lifelong Chicago resident, Bike and his wife, Anne Nordhaus-Bike, run ANB Communications, a full-service communications-consulting firm.

Printed in the United States
5342